LUFTWAFFE OVER THE NORTH

LUFTWAFFE OVER THE NORTH

Episodes in an air war
1939-1943

by
Bill Norman

Leo Cooper

London

First published in 1993 by LEO COOPER
Published in 1997 by Pen & Sword Paperbacks
an imprint of
Pen & Sword Books Ltd
47 Church Street, Barnsley, South Yorkshire S70 2AS

Copyright © Bill Norman 1993, 1997

A CIP catalogue record for this book is available from the British Library

ISBN 0 85052 529 2

Printed in Great Britain by Redwood Books
Trowbridge, Wiltshire

CONTENTS

Introduction

The following pages deal with twenty-four episodes in the air war over the north of England during 1939-1943. Six of the occurrences described deal with air attacks on Tees-side; the remainder are concerned with air operations over a much wider geographical area and embrace the three north-eastern counties.

This is not a *history* of the air war over the north of England during the last war: it is not comprehensive enough for that; nor does it present, examine and evaluate evidence in ways that might be expected of historical analysis. Rather it is a collection of episodes which tell the stories of people who were witnesses to destruction some fifty years ago; ordinary people, who were sometimes called upon to do extraordinary things. Such an approach embraces the facts, but it is also hoped that it provides the reader with a greater sense of immediacy and thus enhanced interest.

Some of the contributors to this volume are ex-*Luftwaffe* aircrew who raided the north some fifty years ago. Their accounts are of particular interest for they show that, despite views current at the time, there were many men *over there* who were as much the victims of time and circumstance as were people *over here*.

Bill Norman,
Guisborough, 1992

Acknowledgments

Since 1984 I have spent much time talking to many people in the north of England who lived through the dangerous — and occasionally exciting — days of World War II and who have been kind enough to invite me into their homes and to share their experiences with me. The list is far too long to include here — but they will know the extent of my gratitude.

However, I must give special mention to Jim Cox (Dormanstown), Albert Farrow (Middlesbrough), and Ernie Reynolds (Wheatley Hill) who answered my initial pleas for help, whose enthusiasm matched — and sometimes exceeded — my own and whose re-collections are liberally spaced throughout these pages. Sadly, Jim Cox died earlier this year and thus never saw the result of the work to which he had contributed so much. Particular acknowledgement is also due to Chris Goss for help given over a number of years and for his collaboration in the writing of episode 13.

Thanks are extended to the following for help generously given: AR Askew; Rudolf Behnisch, ex-II/KG26; S/Ldr George Bennions DFC RAF (Ret'd), ex-41(Spitfire)Sqdn; Les Drinkell; George Hickmott; Stan Hill; Frank Lanning, DFC RAF (Ret'd) ex-141(Defiant)Sqdn; Eugen Lange, ex-1(F)/122; Jeff Moore, ex-604(Beaufighter)Sqdn for his account of crew training; John Moore; Ces. Mowthorpe for details of Moog's flight plans for 9/10 July, 1941; Howard Newbould; Dr. Alfred Price; G/Capt N. Ryder DFC★ CBE RAF (Ret'd), ex-41(Spitfire)Sqdn; John Sherwood; W/Cdr Ted Shipman, AFC RAF (Ret'd) ex-41(Spitfire)Sqdn; Norman Spence; Alan Staveley; S/Ldr Wally Wallens DFC RAF (Ret'd), ex-41(Spitfire)Sqdn; Alf Ward; Peter Watkinson; John Whaley for the Arthur Barratt letter; Mrs Norah Welch; Matt Young, ex-54 Searchlight Regt. RA(TA);

Frau Busekow, Deutsche-Dienststelle, Berlin; the staff of Cleveland County Archives; the staff of Stockton Reference Library; Julia Stephens and John Casey of SBTC Library; RAF Museum, Hendon; Middlesbrough *Evening Gazette* and *The Northern Echo* for permission to use photographs.

Thanks are also due to the following for permission to quote from their published works:
S/Ldr Lewis Brandon, DSO DFC★ [*Night Flyer*, Wm Kimber, 1961]
Air Commodore Alan C. Deere, DSO OBE DFC RAF (Ret'd) [*Nine Lives* Hodder & Stoughton 1959];
Jeremy Howard-Williams [*Night Intruder*, David & Charles, 1976]
MA Liskutin DFC [*Challenge in the Air*, Air Research Pubs, 1987]
Simon Parry [*Intruders Over Britain*, Air Research Pubs, 1987]
WAG Ramsey (ed.) [*The Blitz, then and now*, vol 1 published by After the Battle, 1987] for the use of Oblt. Koch's account of his attack on Hull.
Thorsons Publishing Group for permission to use material from Peter Stahl's *The Diving Eagle*, Wm Kimber, 1984.
The many people who kindly loaned photographs are acknowledged in the following pages; ownership of copyright has been credited in all cases where it is known.

German Air Force terms used in the text
Unit Notation: (eg.8.III/KG26)

The *Luftwaffe Staffel* consisted of nine aircraft and was roughly equivalent to an RAF squadron. *Staffeln* (the plural) were numbered from 1 to 9. Three *Staffeln* made a *Gruppe*, the basic flying unit of the *Luftwaffe*. *Gruppen* were numbered in Roman numerals from I to III. Each *Gruppe* had a headquarters flight (known as a *Stab*) of three aircraft. Thus the full complement of a *Gruppe* was thirty aircraft. Three *Gruppen* made a *Geschwader*, which had its own *Stab* flight of four aircraft. Thus a *geschwader* at full strength had ninety-four aircraft. The role of a *Geschwader* was indicated by a prefix: *Jagd* (JG) were fighters; *Nachtjagd* (NJG) were night-fighters; and *Kampf* (KG) were bombers.

Thus the notation III/KG26 refers to the third *Gruppe* of *Kampfgeschwader* 26. The more specific 8.III/KG26 refers to the eighth *Staffel* of KG26. Because *Staffeln* 7-9 formed *Gruppe* III, the notation 8.III/KG26 was usually abbreviated to 8/KG26.

UNITS
Aufklärungsgruppe Reconnaissance
Kampfgeschwader Bomber
Küstenfliegergruppe Naval Co-operation
Nachtjagdgeschwader Night-fighter
Seenotbereichkommando Air-sea Rescue
Zestörergeschwader Twin-engined fighters

AIRCRAFT
Dornier (Do.)
Focke-Wulfe (Fw.)
Heinkel (He.)
Junkers (Ju.)
Messerschmitt (Me.)

RANKS
Rank RAF equivalent.
Flieger (Flgr.) Aircraftsman 2nd Class (AC2)
Gefreiter (Gefr.) Aircraftsman 1st Class (AC1)
Obergefreiter (Obgfr.) Leading Aircraftsman (LAC)
Hauptgefreiter (Hptgefr.) Corporal (Cpl)
Unteroffizier (Uffz.) Sergeant (Sgt)
Feldwebel (Fw.) Flight Sergeant (F/Sgt)
Oberfeldwebel (Obfw.) Warrant Officer (W/O)
Leutnant (Lt.) Pilot Officer (P/O)
Oberleutnant (Oblt.) Flying Officer (F/O)
Hauptmann (Hptmn.) Flight Lieutenant(F/Lt)
Major (Maj) Squadron Leader (S/Ldr)
Oberstleutnant (Oberstlt.) Wing Commander (W/Cdr)

The code number of each aircraft and its unit is listed where known. In the text, the code follows the aircraft type. The manufacturer's production number of each aircraft (*Werk Nummer*), where known, follows the code.

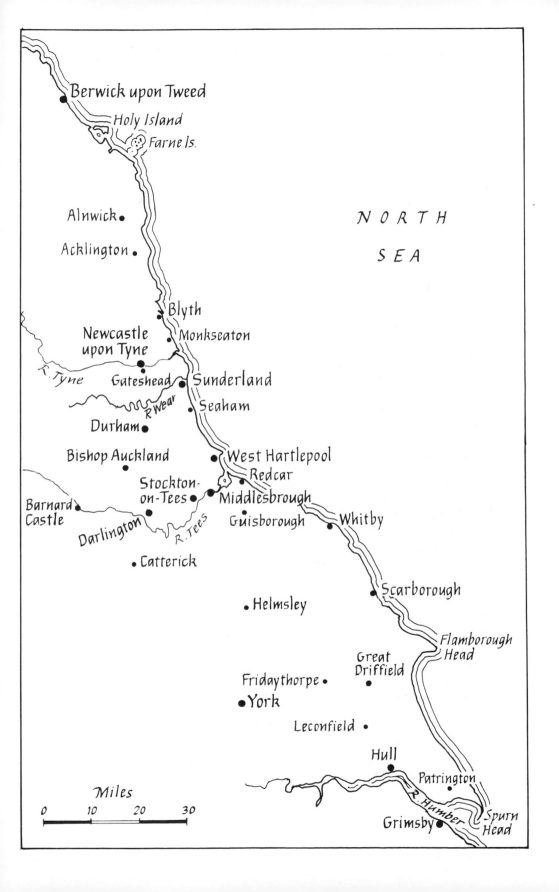

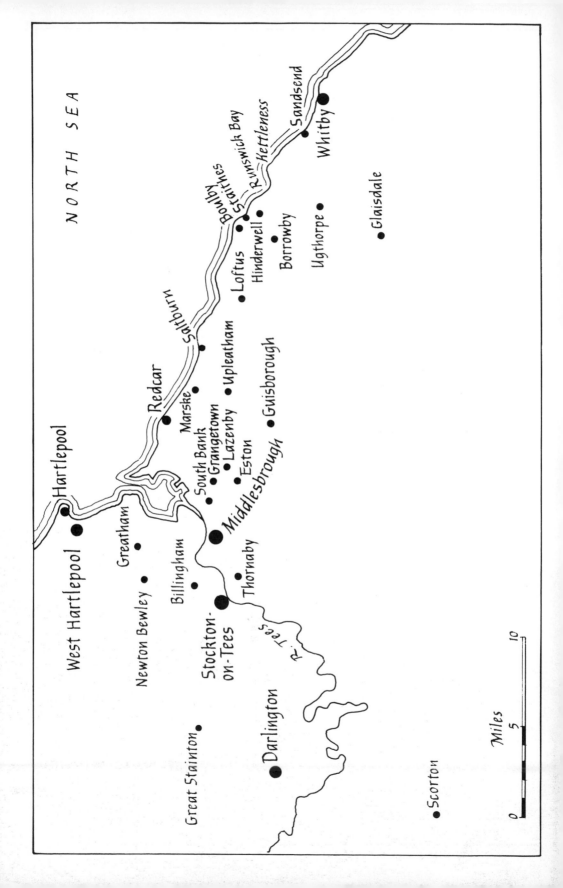

1

PROTECTION AND DECEPTION
(MIDDLESBROUGH, 1938-1940)

Even before the outbreak of war in September, 1939, Tees-side was a centre of industrial and commercial importance. The outbreak of hostilities heightened its significance to the nation's economy and to the war effort. Its heavy industries of iron and steel worked around the clock to forge the basic materials of war; its shipyards built merchant vessels as well as frigates and landing-craft for the Royal Navy; throughout the war years an average of thirty ships per week would clear the river, thus underlining the importance of the Tees as a maritime centre. In addition, local engineering firms and chemical plants were principally engaged in the servicing of war needs. The sheer scale of industrial and maritime activity was bound to make the area a potential target for German bombers.

In 1940 Tees-side's significance was such that it was 'fairly heavily defended' against air attack by thirty heavy guns, which were supplemented by mobile lighter artillery, and a barrage of forty-eight balloons. The North Sea approaches to the area were monitored by three radar stations: Danby Beacon, Goldthorpe (Kettleness), and Shotton (Co. Durham). These provided

The Middlesbrough Ironmasters' District. Not only did the site embrace the Acklam and Britannia group of iron and steelworks of Gjers Mills and Dorman & Long, the north bank of the river provided the location of the Furness shipyards at Haverton Hill (upper right) and the ICI chemical plant at Billingham (upper left). (photo Author's collection)

information on oncoming raiders, not only to static land defences but also to those RAF fighter stations charged with the defence of the area. From the beginning of the conflict there were fighter aircraft based at Catterick, Greatham (a West Hartlepool satellite aerodrome of Catterick), and Scorton, near Richmond. Somewhat farther afield, but in effect covering the approaches from the north and the south, were fighter stations at Usworth (Sunderland), Acklington (Northumberland), and Church Fenton (near York).

There were at least ten observation posts in the Tees-side/Cleveland area. Manned by members of the Royal Observer Corps, their aim was to ensure the accurate identification of aircraft, both friendly and hostile, over-flying specified areas. The posts were sited at West Hartlepool, Seaton Carew, Newton Bewley, Eaglescliffe, Great Ayton, Eston Nab, Redcar, Saltburn, Castleton and Loftus. The Saltburn post perhaps gained more experience than the rest because raiders en route to Tees-side tended to cross in at Huntcliffe; the town also had the rather dubious honour of being the most-bombed town in the North Riding.

Developments in aviation in the decades following the First World War had ensured that in any future conflict every citizen would be a potential target. As early as July, 1937, the British government was sufficiently alarmed by international events to inform local authorities of the importance of making the necessary arrangements to provide for the safety of the civilian population in the event of war breaking out. In Middlesbrough the town council took recognition of the instruction but it was not until February, 1938, that a committee − the Air Raids Precautions' Committee − was formed to meet the specific needs which would be created if the nation went to war with Germany. The newly-formed committee moved fast: by the time the Air Raid Training Centre was opened at St Aidan's Lodge, on 11 July, 1938, the following organizations and procedures had already been set up:

'*A warden organization with an air raid warning system; messenger and information services; anti-gas training; control and reporting; evacuation; billeting; provision of shelters; ambulance; first aid and casualty; fire prevention and static water supply; food control and communal feeding; hospital and maternity services; gas decontamination; war damage and repair service; trades mutual assistance and building trades mutual assistance.*' (*Wm. Lillie:* The History of Middlesbrough, *1968*)

Provision was made with regard to public safety in the event of bombing raids, which were widely anticipated. The Middlesbrough committee ultimately provided communal shelter accommodation for some 80% of the town's population (c.100,000 places), the start of the programme getting underway in September, 1938, when the Munich Crisis gave particular

The brick street shelters would normally withstand the effects of blast - so long as the explosion was not too near. (Location thought to be the Foxheads area of Middlesbrough, near Newport Bridge, c. May 1941). (photo: E. Baxter/Evening Gazette)

impetus. Such forms of protection included trenches, basements in shops and public buildings, and surface shelters of brick and steel, the latter being located in streets and open spaces. In addition, shelter accommodation was provided for 19,000 school-children.

These forms of provision were supplemented by the 'Anderson' and 'Morrison' shelters, which were provided by individual families. A national survey of people's attitudes to the various types of shelter, conducted soon after the outbreak of war, showed that a majority favoured the 'Anderson' — a construction of corrugated steel which was set some three feet into the ground and which had two to three feet of soil on top of it. But, apparently, even these were not without their drawbacks. As one person put it, 'a person is more likely to die from pleurisy by staying in one than by being bombed'. The efficiency of the 'Morrison' — 'little more than a steel table with wire strung around it for use in the home,' — was distrusted by half of the respondents, while others considered brick shelters to be 'about as much use as a sick headache. A breath of wind would knock them down.' That the latter statement was somewhat exaggerated is borne out by the above photograph: like all shelters of the period, those on the surface would not survive a direct hit, but they would usually withstand the effects of blast, so long as the explosion was not too close!

The fear of gas attacks by enemy aircraft prompted the government to issue some thirty million gas-masks at the time of the Munich Crisis in September, 1938. In Middlesbrough 100,000 respirators were assembled and distributed within the space of five days by voluntary labour. Following the declaration of war, on 3 September, 1939, the public were strongly advised to carry their masks at all times, but there was never a legal obligation to do so. In the event, most people did − initially. On the first working day of the war it seemed that everyone was carrying a respirator (usually in a buff-coloured cardboard box slung over the shoulder), but the carrying habit died rapidly after the months of the 'Phoney − and gasless − War'.

At first many places of entertainment refused admission to patrons without masks, but this practice too declined markedly within a few months. It was not until October, 1940, that the government admitted what was by then established practice: that it was no longer necessary to carry gas masks at all times in geographical areas considered to be generally safe from air attacks. However, it was not until 1942 that similar concessions were made in respect of areas considered to be more at risk. In spite of this, many establishments held periodic gas practices for their staff throughout the war, the test usually requiring the employee to work in a mask for fifteen minutes of one day per month.

In Middlesbrough the principal target area in the event of an air raid was widely expected to be the Ironmasters' District, which occupied that rough triangle of land on the south of the Tees loop and between the Newport and Transporter Bridges. Not only did that site embrace the Ayresome and Britannia group of iron and steel plants of Gjers Mills and Dorman, Long − the north bank of the river provided the location for the Furness shipbuilding yards at Haverton Hill and the ICI chemical plants at Billingham. However, in spite of this concentration, it would seem that it was only on relatively rare occasions that such industrial targets were hit during air raids: even then, damage tended to be light. More often than not, bombs intended for the Ironmasters' District fell in open country or they fell − with tragic consequences − on the working-class residential areas that fringed the southern edge of the railway from Newport Bridge to Albert Road.

Possible reasons for such 'near misses' would obviously include the combined efforts of the balloon barrage and the anti-aircraft defences, both of which ensured that the raiders would generally stay at altitudes which would render accurate bombing difficult. However, there were other reasons too. There were, of course, the Blackout Regulations, which ensured that there should be no artificial light exposed to the night sky and thus betray the town's location, and there was also the smoke and haze spewed out by industrial and domestic chimneys.

Later generations were to denounce such atmospheric pollution as being injurious to health, but during wartime there were those who believed that such emissions provided a protective screen which made accurate bombing difficult and which was largely responsible for many bombs going astray. Early in 1941 such 'normal' emissions were supplemented by the distribution of hundreds of oil-burning furnaces − 'like tar machines' − which were spaced at intervals along road-side kerbs at strategic points throughout the area, especially in close proximity to great industrial plants and in and around ICI Billingham. When a raid was impending, it was the responsibility of the Pioneer Corps, acting under the Ministry of Home Security, to ignite the furnaces in designated locations, dependent on wind direction. As they burned, the fires produced large volumes of dense, black smoke to screen the town from the *Luftwaffe*.

If the measure *did* actually save the town from greater destruction, it certainly exacted a price of a different sort. When there were smoke wagons all along Cannon Street 'the air used to be thick'. On one occasion the furnaces issued their palls of smoke over a wide area of Tees-side for thirteen nights in succession. 'Everything was blacked out and people found difficulty in finding their way home. The objectionable smell permeated everything and found its way into houses, even though every crevice in doors and windows had been plugged with papers or rags.'

During the course of the war, various forms of ruse were developed on a national scale to confuse enemy bombers and thus lure bombs to fake targets. Such decoys were located in rural areas away from military and strategic establishments, but close enough to trick raiders into believing that they were bombing their intended objective.

Initially, these tactics applied only to airfields. In October, 1939, the Air Ministry sanctioned the building of two types of dummy airfield: one for daylight use and code-named 'K-Site'; and one for night-time use and code-named 'Q-Site'. By July, 1940, there were some forty 'K' sites in existence nationally and these doubled as 'Q' sites after nightfall. The 'K' site was equipped with full-scale models of aircraft (usually of wood) and buildings, and was manned by some twenty RAF personnel. The 'Q' site simulated a flare-path and the landing lights of an active airfield at night. Such lights would remain lit until raiding aircraft were known to have seen them, then they would be doused in the same way as those on a real airfield in the event of an attack. By the end of 1941 'Q' sites had been attacked 359 times; the real airfields they lured the enemy away from suffered 358 raids.

RAF Thornaby had a 'KQ' site between the Redcar-Grangetown road and Lazenby, on the ground now comprising the west end of ICI Wilton. The

Starfish *bunker at Haughton-le-Skerne, close by the A.66/A.1150 roundabout on the Darlington outer ring road.* (Author)

site covered many acres and had several dummy aircraft positioned near hedges; a wind-sock flew from a staff, and there were several buildings of the type associated with a landing-ground. RAF sentries were posted day and night at the Trunk Road entrance. The site was never attacked by day, but on a number of occasions during night raids on the Tees district a quantity of high-explosives and incendiaries fell close by.

The 'Q' site idea was also applied to the protection of civilian and industrial centres. There were two night-time versions of such schemes: 'QL' (where L=lights) and 'QF' (where F=fire). The former operated as one might have expected a real target to react: the lights were dimmed and extinguished on the approach of a bomber, with the *real target already blacked out.* Thus it was hoped that the bomber would aim at the decoy. The 'QF' system (sometimes called 'Starfish') used decoy fires which were electrically lit when bombs fell in the neighbourhood, the intention being to draw the attack away from the real objective.

It may well be that the idea of arranging decoy fires to mislead raiders, and thus save lives and important strategic installations from destruction, owed its origins to a Saltburn councillor.

Bishop Auckland-born John White was a retired schoolmaster and Chairman of Saltburn and Marske Urban District Council who joined the

Royal Observer Corps in 1937 and who subsequently became head observer of Post Q2, Group 9 (Saltburn). Because most of the raids on Tees-side crossed in by Huntcliffe, and because he was on duty at all hours of the day

and night, White was well placed to study the tactics of the German airmen. He noticed that the usual practice was to drop flares and incendiaries and then follow up with high-explosives on the illuminated areas. He speculated that if masses of inflammable material were to be deposited on large uninhabited areas they could be set ablaze electrically. Thus the enemy might be fooled into thinking that targets had been struck and therefore those fires would become the aiming points of other bombs.

Cllr John White, Chairman of Saltburn and Marske UDC and Head Observer, Post Q2, Group 9 (Saltburn).

Late in 1940 White wrote to the Ministry of Aircraft Production, putting forward his idea and enclosing a map which showed the extensive tracts of marsh land to the east and the north-east of Middlesbrough and Billingham.

Whether or not White was the initiator, Tees-side was chosen as the first area for civilian/military co-operation in this respect. In November, 1940, eight sites were constructed for ICI Billingham and two for Dorman, Long, whose sites on the Lackenby marshes became operational early in the following

year. Decoy lights were also positioned inland towards the Cleveland Hills, while it is believed that on the summit of Eston Hills a 'phoney' military camp was established.

A 'Starfish' site (RAF Upleatham) was located in the field to the south of Sandy Lane, which connects Dunsdale to New Marske. The holed remains of the crew's bunker still stands high in the corner of one of the fields, but the accommodation quarters which stood on the edge of Errington Wood have long since given way to a landscaped car park for walkers' vehicles. The brick bunker of a sister site still stands at Percy Cross, on the moor above Hutton Gate some two

A Royal Observer Corps telephonist on the alert at his Redcar post, November 1940.

miles south-west of Guisborough; the remnants of another can be seen on the hills of Boulby, above Staithes.

In spite of these defences, the wail of sirens was not a rare event: during the period 1939-44 the Tees-side 'Alert' would sound some 480 times. Not all such warnings would culminate in attacks — but there were sufficient of those to cause a significant number of casualties. However, it was generally

The effects of Tees-side's 'normal' smoke-screen can be gauged from this 1940s picture, taken over the north bank of the Tees. In the foreground are Furness shipyards (L) and ICI Billingham (R); Newport Bridge can be seen in upper right, but the Ironmasters' District and the town of Middlesborough are totally masked by industrial smoke. (photo: Author's collection)

believed at the time that, because of the decoy systems then in operation, many of the bombs intended for Tees-side's centres of industry and population exploded harmlessly in the surrounding countryside or on the marshland that flanks the Tees .

EYE-WITNESS

'The site, which was operated by twelve service personnel, had a battery of some thirty to forty 'fires' spread over the field. Each 'fire' consisted of a twelve-foot square metal container full of combustible material, usually rags and wool. Each container was served by a standing tank of oil/paraffin mixture.

When a raid was in progress, the site was activated upon instructions from Thornaby aerodrome. Thornaby controlled the operation — when to start and how many fires to light. When the site was to be operated all duty personnel went into the blockhouse, from where the fires were activated electrically. Once the fires were blazing, water was sometimes released under pressure from an adjacent tank and directed on to the blazing oil/paraffin mixture. This had the effect of simulating explosions.'

George Hickmott, RAF MT, driver Dunsdale *Starfish* site (RAF Upleatham) 1940.

EYE-WITNESS

'We were so unready for war that invasion was very possible. Should invasion take place, large concrete barriers were erected on main roads in

an attempt to slow down the enemy (if he should come); a small opening was left for normal traffic to pass through. In some cases two barriers were erected close together; the opening on one was to the left and the other to the right. You can imagine the difficulties presented to the everyday driver.

When war finally did break out a black-out was introduced. All street lighting and illuminated signs were switched off. There were no shop-window lights: where internal lighting was required, the window had to be suitably covered with black-out material or painted over. Vehicle headlights were fitted with a special mask to direct light downwards; side-lights were covered with two thicknesses of paper to reduce the amount of light — and the rear light (only one in those days) had the normal bulb removed and a smaller one fitted. On public transport, the internal lighting was reduced by removing some of the bulbs, while those remaining were screened.

However, the moon was a problem. It was thought that nothing could be done about that, but eventually an answer was found in a smoke-screen over the town. Hundreds of heavy oil-burning and smoke-producing stoves were made. These were placed at the edge of the footpath and they encircled the town. When a raid was impending, a number of them were ignited (depending on wind direction) and large volumes of black smoke were produced. The moon was blacked out — but so was the town: visibility was nil! Because of the expected large fires, a number of six-inch steel pipelines were laid from the river (and from places where water was plentiful) along the main streets of the town. Valves for the purpose of taking water off were set at intervals. When it became necessary for a pipeline to cross a road it was covered with a ramp to allow traffic to pass over.

You will now realize just how difficult it was for a driver at this time. First the blackout, then the reduced lighting on the vehicles, then the smoke-screen, the concrete barriers and the pipe-lines. It was as if you were driving with your eyes closed.'

Jim Richmond, ambulance/fire engine driver, Billingham UDC Fire Brigade, 1938 onwards.

Starfish bunker off Sandy Lane, New Marske. The decoys were set out in the field beyond the hedge in the foreground. The bunker was originally covered with earth for additional protection. (Author)

2

THE FIRST PRISONERS
(SANDSEND, 17 OCTOBER, 1939)

In the late afternoon of 17 October, 1939, three Spitfires of Green Flight, 41 Squadron, lifted off from RAF Catterick and flew east. On reaching the sea, F/O Peter Blatchford led F/Sgt Ted Shipman and Sgt Albert Harris into a sweeping turn to take the trio south on commencement of their patrol of the North Yorkshire coastline.

Some miles out to sea and to the south-east of the Spitfires' position a Heinkel 111H-1 (F6+PK) of *2/Aufklärungsgruppe 122*, crewed by *Oberfeldwebel* Eugen Lange (pilot), *Unteroffizier* Bernhard Hochstuhl (radio-operator/dorsal-gunner), *Unteroffizier* Hugo Sauer (mechanic/ventral-gunner), and *Leutnant* Joachim Kretschmer (observer), was on a reconnaissance sortie to locate the battle-cruiser HMS *Hood*, believed to be in the Firth of Forth.

The Germans' flight up the north-east coast was the second they had made that afternoon, their first attempt to seek the warship having been curtailed shortly after their arrival in the vicinity of Edinburgh. Eugen Lange recalls:

> 'We reached the Firth of Forth at a height of about 6,000 metres. There was a thick cloud cover at 2,000 metres. How could we get under the cloud without being seen to do a low-level flight to photograph the docks? Before we were decided on tactics...we saw three black dots climbing out of the cloud....There was no alternative, we made off to the east in the hope that the three fighters wouldn't be able to reach our height. After some time, we bravely turned westwards again.'

Soon the Heinkel was travelling north once more, parallel to the coastline and at an altitude of 10,000 feet. Given the vastness of the area over which they were operating the *Luftwaffe* crew might well have expected an uneventful journey – at least until they turned towards the coast for their second approach – but it was not to be.

At approximately 4.30pm Shipman saw the raider some nine miles to seaward of the Whitby coastline over which they were patrolling and, after reporting the sighting to Blatchford, he immediately peeled away in pursuit, his companions following closely behind. Almost at the same time, the Heinkel banked away to the east and dived seawards at full speed in an attempt to escape, but the manoeuvre proved to be of no avail.

Shipman, Harris and Blatchford made their approaches in that order. Shipman was already firing when Hochstuhl, in the dorsal position, opened up with tracer at 450 yards' range. That return fire passed to the Spitfire's port side as the fighter closed to 300 yards, its bullets finding their target and creeping along the Heinkel's fuselage, first to the upper gunner's position and then on to both engines. When Shipman

F/O Peter Blatchford, 41 Squadron, 1940

disengaged he had expended over 2,000 rounds, but "the rear gunner had ceased to fire and both engines had begun to smoke badly."

Harris and Blatchford then took up the engagement, the latter opening fire 400 yards from his target and using up virtually all of his ammunition on his first pass. Such was his eagerness that he approached too fast and overshot, almost colliding with the Heinkel's tail-plane in the process. As he strove hard to avoid that contact there was not the expected reply from the raider's dorsal gun: it was pointing to the sky and there was no sign of Hochstuhl, its operator.

Joachim Kretschmer and Hugo Sauer had both been killed early in the attack — one shot through the head, one through the body — but Hochstuhl was to survive. He had been wounded in the leg and had barely escaped death when bullets scarred the top of his helmet. Lange had enjoyed similar good fortune: the goggles he wore on his forehead were pierced by the bullet that grazed his earphones, but he was unscathed.

However, without any defence and with both engines damaged, the Heinkel was in severe difficulties.

It was Harris who went in to deliver the *coup de grace*, but not before Blatchford had exhausted what remained of his ammunition in a second, more controlled manoeuvre. F6+PK was finished, and the dive that had begun as an evasive measure became a prelude to disaster. However, Shipman was not there to share the moment: believing that his cooling system had been hit, and not relishing the prospect of a watery conclusion to the day's events, he was already on his way home.

The Heinkel glided low over the lumpy sea before smacking down in a cascade of spray some twenty miles east of Whitby. The impact stopped Lange's watch: it was 5.00pm. Blatchford and Harris circled overhead long

EA (Ted) Shipman as a Flight Lieutenant, 1943. (EA Shipman)

enough to see two survivors clamber from the cockpit and slide down the fuselage and on to the wing that was already beginning to settle below the heavy waves.

If the victors speculated on their adversaries' chances of survival at that moment, they cannot have rated the odds particularly high: it was clear that the Heinkel would not stay afloat for long, and the inevitable consequences of the two being cast into heavy seas so far from land did not give grounds for optimism. However, Blatchford did radio the location of the downed fliers to land-based rescue services, but, having done that, there was little else to be done. The Spitfires set course for Catterick, leaving the two to face whatever bleak prospects Fate held in store for them.

As the sound of the Merlins receded, Lange and Hochstuhl must have realized that they did not have much time to dwell upon the seriousness of their situation, but it was Hochstuhl who took the initiative. Although wounded in the leg, it was he who managed to release, inflate and launch their small rubber dinghy in the heavy sea. He managed it not a moment too soon for as they scrambled aboard the tiny boat their aircraft sank below the waves, taking with it the food and drink that they had hoped would sustain them until eventual rescue: a bleak prospect had suddenly become worse.

They spent a most uncomfortable night: wet, bitterly cold and without sleep; all the time paddling with their hands to keep their craft head-on to the rough sea lest a wave should capsize them. At intervals, they fired Very lights, but to no effect. Dawn came, the day passed: there was no sign of rescue and no sight of land.

When darkness fell on the second night Lange was showing increasing signs of exposure and was rapidly losing what strength he had. Hochstuhl, however, managed to keep the dinghy steady. For two hours he also sent up Very lights, but no help came. Even though both the Whitby and the Runswick Bay lifeboats had put to sea in response to Hochstuhl's signals, they could not locate the distressed crew.

Then, on the morning of Thursday, 19 October, dawn brought a glimpse of the cliffs of the Yorkshire coast; they seemed tantalizingly close, but they were too far away for the now-exhausted fliers to paddle. Then Fate smiled kindly upon them: a current caught their rubber boat and carried it to the shore, where the tide lifted it into a rocky cove close to the Lythedale Sands at the foot of the 150-feet cliffs just north of Sandsend village.

Hochstuhl was almost at the end of his strength when he dragged the dinghy and his near-unconscious friend ashore before beginning the very steep climb that would bring help for them both. Painfully, he pulled himself up to the shelf of rock some 40 feet above the shore and which carried the Middlesbrough-Whitby railway line.

LNER Special Constable George Thomas was on duty that day, guarding the entrance to Sandsend tunnel against possible saboteurs. Sometime earlier, as part of his routine, he had walked through the tunnel to the Kettleness side to check with a colleague posted there that all was well. It was as he neared the Sandsend entrance on his return journey that he saw Hochstuhl, in full flying kit, standing near the line and gazing around as if trying to decide which way to go.

As Thomas approached him, Hochstuhl gasped in broken English: 'I am a German flier. My friend is below and needs help. Where am I – near the Firth of Forth?'

Although Hochstuhl had few qualms about being captured, there was a struggle when Thomas went to apprehend him, but only because the flyer wanted to impress upon his would-be captor that Lange was lying below, semi-conscious and helpless. Only when he had been assured that help would be forthcoming did Hochstuhl cease to resist and allow himself to be helped to Sandsend station, some one and a half miles down the track.

When Thomas returned for Lange he was accompanied by Jack Barker, the Lythe duty police constable, and Frank Dring, a Sandsend painter. They found the pilot lying unconscious, perhaps dying, in his water-filled dinghy. The route from the shore to the railway track was treacherous and, given the steepness of the climb and the narrowness of the 'goat track' that had to be negotiated, the group decided to deflate the dinghy and use it as a stretcher. With Barker at the front, Thomas at the back and Frank Dring *underneath* to prevent the dinghy from swaying so much that it would unbalance them and send them all crashing below, they pulled, clawed and occasionally crawled their way to the top. It proved to be a *very* difficult climb.

At Sandsend the Germans were offered food and drink by the station-master's wife but both could take only a few sips of tea and a mouthful of bread. Subsequently police arrived to transport them to Whitby, but before they left Bernhard Hochstuhl gave George Thomas, a heavy smoker, a packet of German cigarettes as a token of his gratitude. Later, Thomas was to state:

'*They were quite decent fellows. One of them said, "I don't know what we're fighting for." I shall not smoke these cigarettes, but I may have one when there is somebody else in charge in Germany and peace is declared.*'

But even though the situation *did* ultimately change he never did smoke them.

On arrival at Whitby both men were taken first to the police-station (where Police Sergeant John Dunning ensured that Lange was placed in a hot bath 'to thaw out') and then to hospital, where they were placed in separate side-wards, each guarded by an Army corporal. On examination, Lange was found to be suffering from frostbite and extreme exposure; Hochstuhl had sustained a shrapnel wound in one leg.

Night Sister Winifred Wilson was one of those responsible for nursing the prisoners. Both created totally different impressions upon her: she found Bernhard Hochstuhl to be 'very charming and highly appreciative of all that was being done for them.' (He gave her his *Luftwaffe* wings as a token of his appreciation) whereas Eugen Lange was 'very stiff and highly suspicious. For example, he would refuse to take his medication until I had sampled it in his presence. I think he thought that we were trying to poison him.'

Suspicious or not, for Lange and Hochstuhl the war was very definitely over: internment, first in England then in Canada, until the end of hostilities awaited them upon release from hospital. But they counted themselves lucky. In one respect they had made history: they were the first prisoners-of-war to be captured on English soil during the Second World War. However, it is likely that they paid scant recognition to that fact, even if they were aware of it. Far more important to them must surely have been that they had been at sea in hostile conditions for 43 hours in a tiny rubber boat without food and without water and they had survived to tell the tale to their grandchildren. Twenty-eight of their fellow-countrymen who were destined to make a landfall of a different sort in Cleveland would *not* live to tell.

Nor would others. Of the three Spitfire pilots, two were destined not to survive the war. Albert Harris was dead within 24 hours of the encounter with the Heinkel: he was killed the following day when the Whitley bomber in which he was a passenger crashed while attempting to take off from

Bernhard Hochstuhl (left) *and Eugen Lange arrive in London.* (Author's collection)

Catterick. Peter Blatchford survived until May, 1943, when, following an engagement with German fighter aircraft, he was forced to ditch in the North Sea, some forty miles from the English coast. Although searches of the area were made, he was never seen again.

Eugen Lange and Bernhard Hochstuhl *did* see most of their rescuers again — when they revisited Sandsend and Whitby in 1979, on the 40th anniversary of their rescue. The only person not present at the reunion was George Thomas: he had died six months earlier. His son took his place.

Postscript:

The above account was first published in the *Whitby Gazette* in October, 1988. As a consequence, I subsequently established contact with Lange and during a telephone conversation on Boxing Day, 1988, he mentioned that he and Bernhard would like to contact the Spitfire pilots who shot them down, if that were possible.

There seemed little room for optimism. I knew that only one, F/Sgt Ted Shipman, had survived the war. If he were still alive, he would be in his eighties. A very slim chance indeed…but where to look? To be truthful, I was so pessimistic that I made little more than a token effort and soon gave up. Then coincidence intervened!

I am not a regular reader of the *Whitby Gazette*, but on 20 October, 1989, (virtually the 50th anniversary of the Heinkel's demise) I bought a copy on impulse. In it was a letter from an ex-Army fellow (then living near Nottingham) reminiscing about being stationed in the town in 1940. Because he made reference to *Luftwaffe* activity, I wrote to him, mentioning my interest in the air war over the north and hoping that he might be able to contribute.

In the event, there was little he could add, but he did pass my letter to a neighbour and friend who had served at Catterick in the early days of the war in the hope that *he* could help. His friend would be in touch, he said.

On 27 November, 1989, the friend wrote to me. It was a most informative letter and the first of many I would receive from him: it was signed by E. A. (Ted) Shipman, Wing Commander, RAF (Retd). The man I had been looking for had introduced himself to me from a totally unexpected direction!

Of course, I am aware that there is always a danger that one can attribute such occurrences to something more than mere coincidence. However, even now I find myself wondering: *if* I had not made that impulsive purchase, and *if* I had not read the letter, and *if* I had not replied to it, and *if* Ted Shipman had not been a friend of the *Gazette*'s contributor, would I ever have established contact with him?

More importantly, perhaps, would three men who once met in less hospitable circumstances over the North Sea 50 years ago now be in correspondence with each other? I rather doubt it, somehow.

When Eugen Lange (left) and Bernhard Hochstuhl returned to England in October 1979 they presented each of their helpers with a small token of appreciation for all that had been done for them. Each received a coloured photograph of the fliers set above a caption printed in silver. The above is taken from one such token.

3

INCIDENT AT BANNIAL FLATT FARM
(WHITBY, 3 FEBRUARY, 1940)

At approximately 6.30am, 3 February, 1940, Heinkel 111 bombers of *KG 26 (Löwen Geschwader)* lifted off from their temporary base in Schleswig, North Germany, and flew due west. They took off in pairs and at three-minute intervals; their task was to locate a British convoy which was southbound from Sweden and believed to be steaming down the north-east coast of England. Any aircraft sighting the convoy was to report its position and to shadow it until the rest of the *geschwader* arrived and a decisive attack could be launched.

One of the aircraft that set out that day was 1H+FM (No. 2323), crewed by *Unteroffiziers* Hermann Wilms (pilot), Rudolf Leushacke (observer), Johann Meyer (flight engineer/ventral-gunner) and Karl Missy (radio-operator/dorsal-gunner). Before the day was over their flight would achieve a measure of historical significance, but two of them would never know.

As the raiders flew out over the forbidding greyness of the North Sea, which was occasionally masked by flurries of snow and wisps of uneven mist that dangled from the base of the low-hanging cloud, three Hurricanes of 'B' Flight, 43 Squadron, stood 'at readiness' at Acklington, Northumberland, the only aerodrome in the north-east sector not snowbound. One of the pilots who shivered in the dispersal hut on that intensely cold February morning was F/Lt Peter Townsend (Hurricane L.2116); the others were F/O 'Tiger' Folkes (L.1723) and Sgt Jim Hallowes (L.1847).

Schleswig was some two and a half hours' flying time from the north-east coast of England. At 9.03am an operator at the North Yorkshire radar station of Danby Beacon reported: 'Two unidentified at 60 miles; approaching at 1,000 feet.' The message was flashed to HQ 13 Group, Fighter Command, at Newcastle, who relayed it to Acklington: 'B' Flight was scrambled.

With Townsend leading, the Hurricanes sped southwards at full throttle; they flew in search formation and at low altitude above the waves to minimize the risk of detection by the enemy. As they did so, faceless voices guided them towards an encounter which would be violent and bloody: 'Vector 180. Bandits off Whitby. Angels one.' Then, two minutes later, 'Raiders attacking unarmed trawler off Whitby.'

F/Lt Peter Townsend, 43 Squadron,
Acklington, 1940.
(photo: Author's collection)

Sgt Jim Hallowes, 43 Squadron,
Acklington, 1940.
(photo: via Alfred Price)

When the fighters arrived, only one raider could be seen. Townsend saw it first — the black, whale-like shape of an He.111 was just below the cloud layer, flying north-northwest above and to starboard of his position. The Hurricanes banked in a climbing turn and closed on their target.

While Hallowes positioned himself to head off any escape attempt, Townsend fired the opening burst. Rudolf Leushacke had time to yell only one warning before he was caught by the first hail of bullets, which peppered the nose-cone in which he was lying: he died instantly. Townsend also hit the starboard engine and when Folkes launched the second attack, from dead astern, that motor was already trailing 'considerable smoke'. As Folkes made his approach, Meyer, who was manning the lower gun position slung on the underbelly, had no time to react before the attacker's gunfire raked along the fuselage and reached him: he was mortally wounded in the stomach and he began to bleed profusely. Karl Missy, in the upper turret, was totally unaware of the fate of his friends as he desperately tried to repulse the attack

29

with the only weapon at his disposal. However, the single MG 15 was no match for the eight Brownings of *one* Hurricane, let alone the combined fire-power of *three* fighters. If he had time to think, he must have realized how hopeless it was, but he did not stop firing, even when the attackers' bullets shattered his legs.

Instinctively, Wilms, the only crew member to escape injury in the attack, knew that the only defence against such odds was the protection that the cloud offered. He pulled hard on the stick and the Heinkel lifted. As it did so, Wilms caught a momentary glimpse of Townsend's Hurricane as it flashed close below the perspex nose-cone where the shattered body of his friend Leushacke lay. Then the Heinkel was enveloped by a blanket of grey.

However, any solace that Wilms and Missy may have drawn from the protective 'invisibility' did not last long: the engines had been hit — the starboard one was out — and failing power made a crash-landing inevitable. Their only hope was to make for the coast, some two miles to the west. When Townsend and Folkes tumbled out of the cloud together, so close that they almost collided, the Heinkel, which had emerged seconds earlier, had lowered its undercarriage and was already turning towards Whitby: behind it there trailed an ever-lengthening, horizontal plume of smoke. But the attackers offered no respite.

The chatter of machine guns and the roar of low-flying aircraft as the crippled raider grazed the cliffs and passed low over the town caused many sightseers to rush out into the streets. What they saw was both dramatic and

Heinkel 111H-3 (1H + FM) lies like a beached whale behind the cottages at Bannial Flatt Farm, nr Whitby. (Northern Echo)

Karl Missy, dorsal-gunner and radio-operator of He.111 1H+FM.
(Photo: Author's collection)

impressive: the crippled Heinkel, riddled with bullet holes and yawing from side to side as Wilms tried desperately to keep aloft on one smoking engine, was gradually sinking earthwards. And as Wilms struggled to delay the inevitable end result, he and Missy could do virtually nothing to resist the impatience of the Hurricanes, which continued to press home attack after attack — one fighter firing at the tail from below, a second firing from above, and the third circling low overhead as if to force the raider even lower. Teenager Francis Cummings, who was on the abbey steps and delivering milk, could only stop and gape, until the metallic ring of spent shell cases falling in the street and the scramble of children anxious for souvenirs distracted him.

By the time it was passing over the Parade the raider was so low that a woman alighting from the Castle Park bus saw Wilms through his cabin window and the swastika on the tail; when it was over Love Lane, where Special Constable Arthur Barratt was at home drinking tea, it was down to 200 feet, 'with three fighters round him like flies round a honeypot'. A crash was clearly imminent and Barratt jumped into his car and followed the route taken by the stricken bomber. Many others, though not all were car owners, followed his example. Among them was 17-year-old J. D. Armstrong, an employee of a Whitby tea company, who borrowed his employer's van and set off in hot pursuit towards Sneaton Castle.

Meanwhile, Wilms, who was now over open country and on the edge of the moors some two miles north of Whitby, struggled to keep control. What he needed was a suitable place to make a landing, but the choice was out of his hands: the ground was very close; close enough for Meyer's dripping blood to trace the aircraft's flight path across the snow-covered fields. Mrs Ruth Smailes, at home at Bannial Flatt Farm, heard the engines and looked out in time to see the doomed Heinkel snap through the telegraph wires suspended in its path and narrowly miss the roof of a barn. Then it was down, its undercarriage collapsing as the aircraft's weight settled upon it.

Circling overhead, the three pilots from Acklington watched with interest while the skidding hulk sprayed snow and mud high into the air as it gouged its way across a field and towards a line of trees and a pair of cottages that blocked its path.

Sixty-eight-year-old Mr H. Steele had been having breakfast in one of the cottages when he had heard the sound of aircraft overhead. He had gone upstairs to look through a window to see what was going on and had been in time to see the crippled Heinkel gliding 'very slowly and very quietly' into the field adjacent to his house. Now, while he stared in stunned amazement, the downed raider was slithering and grinding its way towards him: the only defence against it was a line of sycamore trees that ran close by Steele's house.

Wilms must have been aware of what lay in front of him, but there was

The body of Rudolf Leushacke lies in the snow. (E. Baxter/*Evening Gazette*)

little time to worry, and there was little he could do anyway. Then, the luck that had kept him safe throughout the whole encounter intervened again. His machine was already slowing as it approached the sycamores: when the machine struck the trees the impact was enough to halt further progress; the Heinkel stopped only yards from the cottages.

The first enemy aircraft to crash on English soil during the Second World War was down. Such was the skill of Wilms that Folkes was sufficiently impressed to report later that the landing had been 'carried out under control'.

If the German pilot was shaken by his experience he did not show it. When Special Constable Barratt and a number of farmworkers arrived on the scene some moments later Wilms was crouching in the fuselage and attempting to burn papers. Meyer and Missy lay close by him, both of them clearly in much pain. Barratt, realizing the Intelligence value of such documents, hung down inside the cockpit and grabbed the pilot in an effort to restrain him. But Wilms broke free and completed his task. Then, after marshalling bystanders to help in the removal of his friends from the wreckage, Wilms moved to the shattered nose and fired a Very cartridge into it. However, his attempt to burn his aircraft was unsuccessful: bystanders put out the fire with car-extinguishers and shovelsful of snow.

Karl Missy knew that he had been wounded, but he did not fully appreciate the extent of his injuries until he tried to get out of his seat: his legs were useless. However, the wounds inflicted on his friend were far more serious: Meyer had suffered severe wounds to the stomach and was in extreme pain; he was trapped in the gondola that formed the lower turret and was lying in a pool of his own blood. Missy clumsily lowered himself to the fuselage floor and then made frantic efforts to release his friend, but his own condition meant that he could do little. He heaved himself out of the upper gun position and slid to the ground, leaving Wilms and the bystanders to remove the body of Rudolf Leushacke and then answer Meyer's cries.

Ruth Smailes and Miss A. M. Sanderson were among the first on the scene and they organized the removal of Missy and Meyer to the farmhouse; the body of Leushacke was placed in the cottage coal-house. At the farm, the Smailes's put their charges on a mattress in front of the fire and rendered what First Aid they could; Missy was served with tea and cigarettes, and when it was time for them to leave he attempted to show the gratitude he felt by taking Ruth Smailes's hand and pressing it gently. The two injured crewmen were subsequently taken to the Whitby and District War Memorial Cottage Hospital. Meyer was operated on immediately, but he died later that day; Missy's right leg was found to be so badly mutilated that ultimately it had to be amputated high up.

Among those who looked after Missy during his long stay in hospital was nurse Marion Stainthorpe, who found herself to be 'very frightened about having a German in our midst,' because 'Karl Missy was rather like Rudolf Hess, with dark hair and thick eye-brows.' However, there was little cause for the young nurse to be scared: Missy was in no condition to pose a threat to anyone.

EYE-WITNESS

Dear Will,

By jove I wish you and the lads had been here last Saturday morning to see the aerial battle, it was a sight I shall never forget: I came home for a cup of tea and was sitting at the table drinking it, when, without warning the scene changed to one of the most exciting, shortest, fiercest aerial battles I had ever hoped to see. We heard aeroplanes, and I at once made a dash outside. What a sight met our eyes. There was a great twin-engined bomber just crossing over the top of our house about 200 feet up with three of our fighters round him like flies round a honey pot, and what a barrage they were giving him, poor devil, he hadn't a chance, they dived on him from the top, from underneath, from the side, in fact from every angle possible, firing lead into him all the time. Then the finish, black smoke burst from his tail and he lost height and just skirted over Hill's house and finished up just a couple of yards facing those two houses facing Sleights new road.

Now this is where I come into it. As soon as I saw what the result of the battle was going to be I dashed for my car and was up past Sneaton Castle before the snow settled down when he hit the ground, and reached him just as he came to rest. I, along with some more farm chaps, dashed up to him and I climbed on to the wing. The first Englishman to enter a German plane landing in England since the war started.

When I looked into the cockpit what a sight met my eyes. The Pilot was kneeling down in the bottom of the plane burning his papers, with two of his mates leaning against him, moaning and groaning. I got hold of his collar and pulled him off his papers, but he got clear of me and finished his job of work before I could get to him again. (I was hanging head down in the cockpit.) He came out when the papers were finished and I told someone to look after him, while we lifted his pals out, but in the general excitement they forgot about him and he got to the front of the plane and set fire to the blinking thing while we were struggling with the wounded. Then the thought of bombs etc., going off and putting us all into eternity, so we beat it to a safer distance for a while. I obtained a few fire extinguishers from motor cars which by now had arrived on the scene, and went back with the thought of saving the plane and it took five of the extinguishers and shovels full of snow before we got the fire out and saved it.

By now the Military and fire brigade and ambulances had arrived and took charge of things.

There were, by what we could make out, five men on board, but we could only find four, the front gunner we pulled clear was stone dead, I do not think that he had a whole bone in his body, he got the full brunt of the impact when the plane hit a tree on landing, two more were badly wounded (one since died in Whitby hospital), the other had a foot amputated. The pilot had a few minor wounds and they have taken him away today. I suppose they will find the fifth body under the plane when they dismantle it...

Letter from Special Constable Arthur Barratt to his brother,
4 February, 1940.

There was a big celebration in the Mess of 43 Squadron, Acklington, that evening, for, in addition to the Whitby episode, other Flights of the squadron

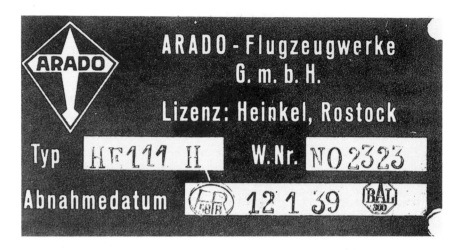

Manufacturer's plate retrieved from He.111 1H+FM by a Whitby souvenir hunter.
(Author's collection)

had scored successes off the Northumberland coast, where other aircraft of KG26 had been intercepted. However, although some thought that the celebration was well-earned, Townsend found himself thinking about the injured crew of *his* Heinkel. When news came through that Meyer had died and that Missy would probably lose a leg, Townsend had an irresistible urge to visit him. Accompanied by other pilots in the squadron who had agreed to join him in buying a wreath for their dead foes, he travelled to Whitby the next day.

When Townsend and Missy met, they did not speak to each other, for neither could speak the other's language. But had that not been the case, what could they have said that would have been meaningful? Townsend merely stood by the bed in which Missy lay and simply extended his hand, not knowing what the response would be. Missy was weak, perhaps dying, but he took Townsend's hand in both of his and clasped it until it hurt. As he did so, the sadness in his eyes stamped itself on Townsend's mind; perhaps in that moment each understood the other. As Missy sank back on his pillow, Townsend handed him a bag of oranges and a tin of fifty Player's cigarettes that he had taken for him, and then he left.

The bodies of Rudolf Leushacke and Johann Meyer were subsequently removed to Catterick, where they were buried with full military honours; on each coffin there was a wreath 'From 43 Squadron, with sympathy.' The original intention had been to bury them locally, but such was the intensity of feeling against German fliers 'who attacked defenceless fishing vessels' that it was necessary to seek an alternative.

Postscript:

Hermann Wilms was taken to an internment camp and survived the war: he died in December, 1974, in Kaufbeuren. Karl Missy was repatriated to his home town of Rheydt in October, 1943, as part of a POW exchange. It was there that Peter Townsend renewed his acquaintance with his old adversary when he made a special trip to the German town in 1969. Missy survived Wilms by seven years and died in 1981 at the age of 69. 'Tiger' Folkes was dead within a month of the Whitby incident: his aircraft crashed into the North Sea off Wick during a convoy patrol and he was never seen again. Jim Hallowes survived the war and left the RAF in 1956 with the retained rank of Wing Commander: he died in 1987. Peter Townsend also survived the war. In 1944 he was appointed Equerry to King George VI, a post that he held until the King's death in 1952. He retired from the RAF in 1956 with the rank of Group Captain and settled in France, where he wrote his autobiography *Duel of Eagles*, which includes an account of the events of 3 February, 1940. He died in June 1995.

In June, 1945, the (then) North Riding County Council erected a plaque to commemorate the incident. It can be seen on a stone pillar at Sleights Lane End, some three miles north of Whitby, at the junction of the A171 and A169. The 50th Anniversary of the incident passed unnoticed.

The crash site 50 years on. The Heinkel (1H+FM) came to rest in the gap in the line of trees to the left. (Author)

Inset: In June 1945 the North Riding County Council erected a plaque close by to commemorate the incident. (Author)

4

A SPITFIRE PILOT'S SEA ADVENTURE
(REDCAR, 3 APRIL, 1940)

In February, 1940, the RAF took possession of a grass airstrip at Greatham, County Durham, and renamed it RAF West Hartlepool. The airstrip was to serve as a satellite of Catterick aerodrome, some 30 miles to the south-west, and was to be the daytime base for (usually) four fighter aircraft engaged on coastal patrol and convoy protection duties, the harassment of east coast shipping by German bombers having become an established practice by the early months of 1940. The first aircraft to be placed there on detachment were Spitfires of 41 Squadron. On Wednesday, 3 April, 1940, the RAF lost its first Spitfire to the guns of the *Luftwaffe*; the same aircraft was the first British fighter to be shot down while protecting the shores of England during the Second World War; it was Spitfire N.3114 of 41 Squadron.

April 1940. Spitfires taking off from Greatham (RAF West Hartlepool), Co. Durham, prior to patrol over the North Sea. (Author's collection)

Spitfire pilots of 41 Squadron, c. December 1940. Norman Ryder is standing in the front row, 2nd from the left. (Author's collection)

The day had broken overcast and dull. Over the North Sea the cloud base was down to 600 feet and visibility, reduced by a combination of mist and rain, was down to 3-4 miles. Such conditions posed few problems for fishermen and by mid-morning a number of drifters and trawlers from Scarborough and other north-east ports were some miles off shore and busily engaged in the business they knew best. On land, however, the weather conditions were the subject of more serious consideration and at Catterick there were those who openly speculated on the wisdom of mounting a routine patrol at all that morning. In the event, the matter was taken out of their hands when it was reported that a German bomber was attacking shipping some four miles north of Whitby. Flt/Lt Norman Ryder was 'scrambled' from Greatham at 12.21pm. Seventeen minutes later he launched his attack.

After crossing out over Redcar, Ryder sped south-east towards an eventual rendezvous with a Heinkel 111 H-3 (1H+AC) of *Stab* II/KG26 commanded by *Gruppenkommandeur Oberstleutnant* Hans Hefele and crewed by *Leutnant* Rudolf Behnisch (pilot), *Leutnant* Georg Kempe (observer), *Unteroffizier* Albert Weber (radio operator) and *Unteroffizier* Alfred Bächle (mechanic).

The Heinkel had taken off three hours earlier from its base at

39

January 1940: Rudolf Behnisch (centre) poses with another crew alongside He.111 1H+AC. Uffz Albert Bachle is second from the right. (R. Behnisch)

Lubeck-Blankansee on an armed reconnaissance sortie against British shipping. Fifty years on, Rudolf Behnisch recalled that:

> 'The armed reconnaissance ("bewaffnete Aufklärung") was timed in such a way that several planes showed up at the same time at different places along the British coast... a low cloud-base was an absolute·necessity. Flying over British land was strictly forbidden at the time.
>
> We made out a small convoy and we attacked right away the biggest one of them. We had to fly directly through the fire that came up from the boats.
>
> I am not sure whether our bomb hit the boat, but I was pretty sure that I was hit in my left engine. As a result, the electricity system failed and I could not change the prop blades from two- to one-engine flying position. As a result, I flew near stalling speed and could not climb into the protecting clouds. Another handicap: a hole in the port wing was so wide and caused such high wind resistance that I could not steer a straight course. The aircraft

drifted to the left in spite of trimming — a fact that I hoped to overcome by having the crew members pump the fuel by hand from the port wing to the starboard tanks.

All those considerations became useless when the radio operator, Uffz Weber, called out: "British fighter plane approaching from left behind".'

When Ryder made his interception, some fifteen miles north-east of Whitby and four miles off the coast, it was immediately apparent that the raider was already in trouble: its port engine was 'badly disabled. Possibly completely out of action' and the aircraft was flying at reduced speed at 400 feet, just below the cloud base. Ryder had to throttle back and circle in order to slow down before attacking from astern. The raider's vulnerability was emphasized as Ryder began his own slowing manoeuvres: the Heinkel slanted, as if to climb, but it could make little headway. There was no other form of evasive action after that.

Prior to his first attack, Ryder passed ahead of his quarry. It was then that Hefele, lying on the mat behind the front gun, fired a burst which, Behnisch noted, 'covered the Spitfire quite well'. Ryder heard two bangs below his engine as bullets found their target, but he chose to ignore them; moments later his own six-second reply found the Heinkel's starboard engine. As Behnisch was later to describe:

'The whole of his eight machine guns went into the right wing and I had to shut down the right motor. Nothing else to do but go into the sea.'

Ryder broke away left and returned to attack as he continued his port turn. But on his second approach he saw that the Heinkel's starboard engine was emitting a combination of grey and black smoke and there was a momentary flash of flame from the spinner. The enemy aircraft was steadily losing height and thus Ryder refrained from firing. Instead, he positioned himself to starboard of his quarry and watched it descend seawards.

The crew of the Scarborough drifter *Silver Line* skippered by Bill Watkinson of Filey, had watched the encounter with excited interest and, perhaps, some trepidation. Three weeks earlier skipper Watkinson had been dive-bombed by a raider and, although no hits had been registered on that occasion, it was not an experience that he wanted repeated. Nor did his brother Tom: *he* was already manning the Lewis gun — just in case.

When the Heinkel made its low-level approach towards them, the fishermen feared the worst. However, even though the raider's armament was awesome compared with their own meagre resources, the crew of *Silver Line* intended to make a fight of it. As the bomber passed low over them, Tom Watkinson 'let go' with the Lewis gun and, as the Germans were later to confirm, at least ten strikes were made, including one which wounded Kempe in the

The Scarborough drifter Silver Line *(SH.50) draws alongside the stricken Heinkel (1H+AC) while Ryder's crippled Spitfire makes its way northwards. An artist's impression by John Moore. (Author)*

head. In spite of this there was no return fire from the crippled aircraft as it glided tail down towards ultimate oblivion: ditching was imminent and the crew were bracing themselves for the impact, which came with a rasping smack, a dull roar and a cascading wall of water.

The stricken hull could not cope easily with the seven-foot swell and immediately started to ship water. It began to sink as the five-man crew evacuated the fuselage and scrambled on to the wing. With some urgency, two members released the aircraft dinghy and tried to float it, only to find it bullet-holed and useless.

At about that time the circling Spitfire passed close by, its pilot waving in salute: it was then then Bächle noticed that the fighter was trailing white fluid and Behnisch thought he saw a lick of flame.

By this time *Silver Line* was steaming to the aid of the German fliers, but the vessel was still some distance away when the nose of the Heinkel dipped more steeply below the waves, casting its crew into the water and leaving only the tail visible to mark the starting point of the aircraft's journey to the sea bed. It was then that Behnisch discovered that his lifejacket would not hold air and so he had to climb on to the tail, a temporary buoy on which to cling until the drifter was close enough to strike out for.

As *Silver Line* drew alongside and ropes were lowered, the downed airmen might well have wondered about the reception they would get. Certainly the Scarborough men were intent on helping, 'for no fisherman can leave another to drown, no matter what he has done,' but they had decided against taking chances. They had noticed that one of the Germans was wearing a pistol. Thus the possibility of a 'take-over' bid by the enemy did not seem to be idle conjecture and so while his mates plucked the airmen from the sea, one by one, a Scarborough crewman kept a rifle at the ready and warned that 'if they brought firearms on board then they would not live a minute.' The pistol was handed over without incident.

As *Silver Line* made its way towards Scarborough the airmen proved to be very docile prisoners; they were also very suspicious and somewhat apprehensive about their reception on reaching port. When their rescuers assured them that they would be well treated as POWs in England, they cheered up and their (now smiling) commander instructed skipper Watkinson to 'make for England. We never wanted to fight you, anyway!'

En route, Rudolf Behnisch gave Bob Watkinson his gold signet ring as an

Rudolf Behnisch II/KG26
January 1940 (R. Behnisch)

Uffz A. Bächle II/KG26. January 1940
(R. Behnisch)

expression of his gratitude for not being left to drown; another German gave Tom Watkinson a watch for the same reason.

Ryder, having watched the rescue as he circled overhead, set course for home. However, he had not travelled far before he noticed that the oil temperature gauge was rising alarmingly. Even as he advised Control that he was in trouble the combination of oil fumes and rapidly rising temperature made the cockpit a most uncomfortable place to be. He was some 15 miles off Redcar and it was becoming increasingly clear that his machine was not going to take him there. Catterick spelled out the options by advising him to make for the coast or bale out or ditch in the sea, but Ryder cannot have found such statements of the obvious particularly helpful. As he pondered what to do next, he spied the trawler *Alaska* and began to circle it.

After some deliberation, he realized there was little prospect of reaching land; at the same time, he felt that the cloud was too low for him to bale out with safety, even if he could gain sufficient height. He decided to ditch close to the trawler, just as his victim had done minutes earlier, and began his approach. However, when he was fifty feet above the waves, and with *Alaska* still half a mile away, Ryder's engine failed just as he slid open the hood. The Spitfire fell sharply into the heavy swell and ploughed into a seven-foot wall of water.

The sudden deceleration catapulted him forward and he was knocked unconscious: he regained his senses only when his aircraft started to sink beneath the waves and the cold water washed over him. When he opened his eyes, both he and his aircraft were under water. As he sat strapped in his seat his machine began its slide to the sea bed.

As the Spitfire settled further below the surface and the angle of descent became steeper, the enveloping 'greenness' began its change to a darker hue. Ryder realized that it was time to get out. He undid his straps and stood on his seat, but instead of floating free, he discovered that he was still going downwards: his aircraft was sinking at a steeper angle and his parachute had snagged itself under the sliding hood; he could not move and the once attractive greenness was beginning to change to a more sombre colour.

By this time he was swallowing water and yet his mind remained clear enough to realize the cause of his difficulty. He climbed back into the cockpit and attempted to free his parachute from its snare. It was then that he realized just how much darker it was getting. When he finally did break free it was *very* dark and he could only just make out the silhouette of the Spitfire's tail as it passed in front of his face. Then he struck out for the surface. Although he still had his parachute strapped to him he finally managed to dog-paddle his way upwards. But his problems were by no means over.

When he emerged into daylight Ryder found that his Mae West would not inflate and that the combined weight of his parachute and his saturated flying clothes made him too heavy to ride the swell. Most of the time the waves were breaking *over* him, which meant that he could catch only an occasional breath. He needed to shed some weight — and his parachute was the obvious candidate.

Although his strength had been sapped by his earlier efforts, Ryder, continually buffeted and swamped by the waves, eventually managed to release himself from the burden which had threatened to drag him down. But as the saturated bundle began to drift away, Ryder began to sink: ironically, it had been the parachute that had been keeping him afloat; without its support he would surely go under. In one desperate lunge, he grabbed his only chance of survival and, weak and exhausted as he most certainly was, hung on grimly while the seas continued to break over him and deny him more than the minimum intake of air to sustain life.

Norman Ryder 41 Squadron November 1940.
(N. Ryder)

He was weakening and he was aware of it. Then, when all seemed lost, he caught a momentary glimpse of the trawler and heard shouts of encouragement. As another roller swamped him, something touched his arm. Instinctively, he grabbed it and held on as best he could. Then he felt strong hands lifting him.

As *Alaska* chugged its way westwards towards Hartlepool and *Silver Line* made for Scarborough, word went out that the fliers were safe and the search that Catterick had initiated when Ryder lost contact was called off. Twelve miles east of Hartlepool, the town's lifeboat, *Princess Royal*, turned for home; close by the Royal Navy destroyer *H.92* resumed its patrol duties; among the fishing boats that were making for the coast as *H.92* made out to sea were several trawlers whose crews had left port to answer the call for help when help was needed.

When the Whitby fishing vessel *Eastern Morn* reached port in the early afternoon to report that shipping was under attack some miles off shore the drama was already over: Ryder was on his way to Hartlepool and would soon rejoin his squadron; it would, however, be a different story for his antagonists.

Silver Line landed them at Scarborough Quay that evening. Kempe was removed to the hospital by a waiting ambulance, the rest were taken to the police station where they were fed before being collected by military personnel who escorted them to Burniston Barracks prior to interrogation and eventual internment.

On 6 April, 1940, the crew of *Silver Line* were received at Scarborough

Some of the crew of the Scarborough drifter Silver Line *pose with one of the statuettes with which each was presented in recognition of his part in the events of 3 April 1940. L to R: Chas. Hunter (gun-loader); Ted Robinson; Bill Watkinson (skipper); Tom Watkinson (gunner); Bob Watkinson (mate). Other members of the crew were: A. Barley (engineer); W.G. Cole (2nd engineer); D. Holmes (cook).* (P. Watkinson)

Town Hall by the Mayor, when their part in the bringing down of the Heinkel and then rescuing its crew was officially recognized by the presentation of a silver statuette of a lifeboatman to each of them. (The crew of *Silver Line* always believed that they had put paid to the raider and they quoted one of the Germans as confirming this. However, they refused to contest the RAF's claim to the victory.) After leaving the Mayor's office they kept a promise made to a foreign foe three days earlier: they visited the injured Kempe in hospital and presented him with gifts of oranges and cigarettes.

Postscript:

Norman Ryder, perhaps the only flier to be saved by parachute after 'baling out' of a submerged aircraft, went on to fight in the Battle of Britain. Late in 1941, while leading 485 Squadron, he was shot down by flak over the French coast. He crashed on the beach near Calais and spent the rest of the war as a POW. He retired from the RAF in 1960, having reached the rank of Group Captain. He died in America in 1995. *Alaska*, a fishing vessel of 21 gross registered tonnage, struck a mine off Easington, County Durham, on 25 March, 1941, and sank: it is not known how its crew fared. All of the German crew survived the war and returned home, Behnisch to study languages at the University of Hamburg. On 3 April, 1990, Rudolf Behenisch kept a promise he made to himself 40 years earlier, when he revisited Scarborough. The crew of *Silver Line* are now dead, but on 3 April, 1990, the son of Bob Watkinson met Rudolf Behenisch at an emotional meeting in Bridlington.

Nearly fifty years after the Ryder incident, the Watkinson family had another brush with the *Luftwaffe*. On 8 January, 1988, Bob Watkinson's grandson, Peter, as skipper of a modern *Silver Line*, netted a ten-foot-long, 1,500lb land mine while fishing 15 miles off Flamborough Head. It was believed to have been jettisoned during the Second World War by a German bomber returning from a raid over England. Peter towed his 'catch' to the comparatively shallow Smithwick Sands, some three miles off Bridlington, where a bomb disposal team from Portsmouth subsequently despatched it in a controlled explosion.

5

THE FIRST BOMBS FALL
(SOUTH BANK AND GRANGETOWN,
25 MAY, 1940)

On the night of 24/25 May, 1940, He.111s of KG27, operating from bases in western Germany, launched a series of attacks against targets in east and north-east England. At 1.41am on Saturday, 25 May, 1940, Tees-side entered the record books of the Second World War when the first German bombs to be dropped on an industrial target in this country during that conflict fell on the Cargo Fleet Ironworks at South Bank and on the Dorman, Long south steel plant at Grangetown. The same bombs also produced the first civilian casualties to result from a bombing raid over England during the 1939-45 period, although one month earlier two civilians had been killed and 150 injured when a German mine-laying Heinkel 111 had crashed into houses at Clacton-on-Sea.

When it came, that first attack was totally unexpected. Most people were asleep in their beds: there had been no siren call and no sound of gunfire, either of which would have alerted the unsuspecting that an attack was pending. Thus, for those who were still awake that night, the sound of a high-flying aircraft overhead gave no cause for alarm: it was only when searchlights began to scan the sky that suspicions were aroused. By then, the raider was gliding down to a level where it would be low enough to be seen by eye-witnesses and from where it would release the first of its bombs.

A party of motorists in the area had *their* suspicions aroused when they saw a solitary searchlight sweeping the skies. One of the travellers subsequently recalled that:

'*Suddenly the sky was lit up by beams coming from all directions. We thought that something might be happening so we stopped the car and pulled back the sunshine roof. We heard the noise of the plane, and then we saw blinding flashes coming from the direction of the works and heard the noises of terrific explosions.*

This was something that we had not expected so we started up the car and made all speed to tell the police.'

They did not need to travel far. Such was their anxiety to notify the authorities that they set off driving with their car lights on – until a policeman stopped *them* and no doubt told them in no uncertain terms that there was a black-out in force and a raid in progress!

Fourteen small-calibre bombs (estimated to have been between 50lbs-60lbs each) were released in a line which stretched from Cargo Fleet works to Dorman's Grangetown plant. The first landed just inside the perimeter fence of the Fleet complex and caused more inconvenience than damage when it deposited debris on the Middlesbrough-South Bank road. The second burst almost opposite the first, on the south side of the road, the blast being powerful enough to shatter windows in Pine Street and in Elm Street, Cargo Fleet. The third struck the works' travelling crane shed, damaging the structure but not the plant. The fourth struck waste ground to the east of the works' offices, blowing in all of the windows on that side of the building and extensively damaging windows in a row of houses facing that waste ground. The fifth fell by the shelters near to the Tees-side Rail-less Traction Board (TRTB) depot, causing damage to gas and electricity mains and some damage to Post Office cables. The sixth and seventh fell close to the road bridge over the railway, causing no damage whatsoever but nevertheless prompting a number of motorists on their way home from a dance in Redcar to vacate their vehicles and dive into a nearby ditch! The eighth exploded at the rear of Aire Street, South Bank, where it demolished a home-made shelter and extensively damaged the rear premises of five houses. The ninth made a crater in the pitch of South Bank Football Club, Normanby Road. The

Clearance squads at work at the rear of Aire Street, South Bank, 25 May 1940.

tenth dropped in an allotment on Mundy Street and the eleventh struck the slag tip opposite Middlesbrough Road: neither caused damage. Two dropped close to the Eston Council offices on Eston Road, without any great effect. The last bomb dropped close to Dorman's south steel plant, where it caused no damage to plant but did result in injuries to eight workers who were sitting in a weigh cabin some twenty feet from the explosion. John Bidwell (42), Trevor Evans ('middle aged') and Jonathan Jones (19) were injured sufficiently to be detained in hospital, but the area and its people had been let off exceptionally lightly.

The lack of serious casualties and severe damage to property was due to exceedingly good luck, for most of the explosives fell in open areas. Had the bombs been released fractionally earlier or later than they were the result might well have been much worse. The next morning, people were asking why there had been no warning and why anti-aircraft defences had not taken action, but the findings of official enquiries were not publicized. It was claimed, however, that the raider had been driven off by RAF machines "which had quickly arrived on the scene" but there is some cause to doubt the claim. By the time would-be defenders arrived, the bombing had stopped and the raider had gone. All that the fighters could do was to make a gesture and thus the "British machines were seen speeding out to sea, as if in chase of the raider."

In fact, such defenders could do little else. Night-time interceptions were very much a lottery in the early days of the war and rarely produced positive results. Night-fighter pilots would have to wait for another two years — and for the perfection of airborne radar, particularly when used in the Beaufighter — before they would be able to take effective action against raiders.

In the absence of the siren warning, most people in the target area found that the crash of the first bombs was the signal to rush to the shelters. They might well have been highly critical of the authorities as they made their dash for safety, but there was one family in South Bank who would have cause to be grateful for such apparent inefficiency.

The bomb that landed at the rear of Aire Street exploded within five yards of the terrace of houses. The walls, doors, out-houses and sculleries were blasted in and every window and frame was smashed. The Walkington family were in their home when the bomb struck, and though the house suffered the blast effects experienced by adjacent buildings, the family survived without injury. The bomb had landed on the soft earth covering of their home-made shelter: had the siren given warning they would have been taking refuge there and probably would have been killed.

One of the interesting aspects of the attack was that thousands of people living in adjoining areas slept through it and were totally unaware that it had taken place at all until they were told many hours later. One who slept through it all was the Walkington's 10-year-old daughter, Margaret: she was discovered in her small bedroom, sleeping in a bed which was covered with broken glass and splintered woodwork. Mrs J. Sproul, who kept a sweet-shop in Aire Street, reacted somewhat differently to the first explosions. When she and her husband heard the bombs drop, "and a terrific noise it was, and all the bedroom window was blown on to a table near my bed, *we immediately got out of bed!* It was a terrible experience, but everyone kept cool."

Testimonies to people's coolness were to come from a number of quarters, including the Superintendent of Police who was moved to comment that everyone had done as they were requested "without fuss or panic; they were marvellous" while the ARP chief for the district noted with satisfaction that his organization had functioned with the smoothness of a practice. He went on to state that:

"All posts were fully manned, and wardens and police were out reporting damage in very quick time. Rescue and Demolition were soon in action and working well."

It was a sentiment that would be voiced on a number of occasions during the following two years: for Tees-side the 'Phoney War' was over and for many of the area's inhabitants Fate was destined not to be kind.

6

A LUFTWAFFE OBSERVER REMEMBERS (MIDDLESBROUGH AND HULL, 1 JULY, 1940)

On 1 July, 1940, Heinkel 111 (5J+EL) of 3/KG4 was detailed to attack the chemical works at Middlesbrough. The aircraft, crewed by *Oberleutnant Zur See* F-K Koch, *Oberfeldwebels* H. Raisbach and R. Ernst, and *Feldwebel* A. Weber, *did* reach its intended target, but the town was spared the possibility of a measure of destruction when the *Luftwaffe* spotted Spitfires in the area. Although they had not been sighted by the defenders, the German fliers thought it prudent to fly to Hull — their secondary target.

Koch's description of the events of that day is of interest for a number of reasons: its clear demonstration of the *Luftwaffe*'s ignorance of the effectiveness of British radar at that time; the insight it offers into the daylight-bombing tactics practised by the *Luftwaffe* crews in the early days of the war on those occasions when they were far from home and without fighter cover; and, for those old enough to remember, it offers an additional explanation of the constant sounding of the 'Alert' in the early days of the conflict — a precaution which, it seems, sometimes owed as much to the vacillations of a raider unable to make up his mind regarding his target as it did, perhaps, to more purposeful crews whose approach was more direct.

'*On July 1, 1940, our* Gruppe *for the first time was ordered to perform a daylight attack against industrial targets. Each of our three squadrons had to nominate one crew. In our squadron I volunteered for this raid and was lucky enough to get the last serviceable aircraft that, unfortunately, also became unserviceable while performing the pre-take-off check. However, the indefatigable ground crew enabled us to take off with two hours' delay.*
MISSION ORDER: *High-level attack against targets of the British war industry, in this particular case the chemical works at Middlesbrough, with secondary target, the oil works at Hull. All decisions in connection with the mode of attack or choice of target were left to my own discretion with the only limitation that the mission was to be broken off if the cloud cover 100 kilometres before the coast was less than the five-tenths.*
EXECUTION: *With the Juist beacon as a navigational aid, the course*

Crew member on alert in the nose-cone of a He.111 Taylor Library

was set on Flamborough Head. The weather conditions as stipulated for the performance of the mission seemed not to meet the requirements; however, after having learned from my wireless-operator that both the other aircraft had broken off their mission for one reason or the other , I felt obliged to press home my attack even under less favourable conditions. A little less than 100 kilometres from the coast a thin strato-layer indicated that the cloud cover hoped for could be expected. In fact, the cloud cover with a 4,500 metre ceiling allowed for an approach within clouds.

At about 1630 hours, German summer time, we descended and broke clouds exactly where I was supposed to be: just south of Flamborough Head. However, on account of the weather situation, I decided not to fly to Middlesbrough but to turn southwards where the cloud cover seemed to become thicker which, moreover, was in accordance with the weather forecast.

Just north of the estuary of the Humber river clouds were broken and the town of Hull lay in front of us under a nearly spotless blue sky. Shortly after having left the cloud cover my wireless operator reported three Spitfires. In order not to be spotted by them, I turned back into the clouds, setting course on Middlesbrough. After a twenty-minute flight the clouds broke here, too, and became thin and hazy. While I was pondering whether I should disregard the unfavourable weather conditions, again Spitfires were reported in sight — six of them flying at the same altitude, but apparently they had not sighted us. As before, it seemed mere chance to me that these fighters crossed our way and purpose.

At that time I did not know what I learned afterwards about the radar-directed fighter control of the RAF. My ignorance in this respect was the reason for the misinterpretation of the prevailing situation since my further moves were based on the assumption that our meeting the fighters was merely incidental and not the result of radar-controlled direction. Therefore, I decided to fly an eastwards course for about ten minutes, then, at a safe distance parallel to the coastline up to the latitude of Hull. I intended to remain

53

within the clouds up to the coast, then leave the clouds in order to orientate myself for the subsequent attack. Due to the short interval between our appearance and the attack, I hoped to outwit the air raid warning and fighter interception...

Navigation was exact. When leaving the clouds we hit the coastline. Suddenly I spotted an airfield with a number of light-coloured planes. In a sudden impulse I felt tempted to attack this surprise dream target. The apparent negligence of the usual camouflage, however, made me wary that it might be a mock-airfield and I resisted the temptation.

We now left cloud cover at about 5,500 metres. Hull and the nearby target lay under a blue sky so that our arrival over this area undoubtedly must have caught the attention of the defence forces. Some scattered clouds at about 4,000 metres, which were in my way for the adjustment of my bomb-sight, caused me to lose height. Shortly before reaching the town I turned in for the final target run on a course of 240 degrees when my wireless-operator again reported three Spitfires in sight. I had to make a quick decision: either to return into the cloud cover or to continue the target run. Since it was doubtful whether a return might be possible, I decided to carry on with what I was here for: to bomb the oil tanks.

For the whole time we were in the target area we were subjected to AA fire which was extremely unpleasant during the final approach, because, for best results I had to keep altitude, speed and course constant, thus facilitating the AA in their correction. In fact, one of the shell fragments entered our cockpit and damaged part of my instrument panel. In spite of these irritations we continued our target run up to the moment when I dropped my bombs. In this connection I have to praise the outstanding performance of my pilot, who executed my course corrections with calmness and coolness in an absolutely perfect manner.

After I had released the bombs, I ordered the pilot to perform a steep turn and to descend at the highest allowable speed. When I saw the twelve 50kg bombs had crossed the tank installations with several direct hits, causing explosions and fire, I tried to set up a coded mission report because I doubted that I would be able to do it later.

Still several thousand metres high, we reached the Humber estuary when the Spitfires circled in for their first attack. Since the time we flew in the AA fire zone, they had waited at a safer distance, but now they closed in for attack. Although lying in the front part of the aircraft, manning the forward gun, I was able to follow the events through our intercom. Already, after the first machine-gun bursts of my wireless-operator in the upper rear gun position, he had a malfunction of his gun, leaving us without any defensive means to the rear. From this moment on the fighters could carry out their attacks unhindered and at short range — with corresponding results. One after the other made his run and poured out the projectiles of the eight guns of each Spitfire.

Each time a Spitfire launched an attack, a noisy stream of bullets rushed through our aircraft. At first the instrument panel was shot to pieces, then one engine put out of action. Next, the landing gear became unlatched and fell down, and the flaps came off. After the second engine was put out of action and the starboard ailerons had been shot away, the Spitfires left the crippled victim and returned to their base. The pilot, left without instruments and flaps and ailerons, damaged rudder and propellers which could not be feathered, struggled with his controls, miraculously managing to keep the aircraft flying.

Now, once the continuing rattling noise of the bullets had ceased, it became deadly still in the aircraft. My pilot asked me to guess speed and altitude, since he had no instruments and was fully occupied in his struggle with the controls. To ensure our survival immediately after the crash, it was imperative to activate our rubber dinghy that was fastened in the rear behind a steel plate. I called the mechanic who answered that the wireless-operator had been hit several times and was likely to be dead, and he himself was hit in the leg and buttocks, yet still cracking a joke about his inglorious end.

I went back and realized that we would not get the dinghy out of there because the dead wireless-operator blocked the upper exit. I pulled the rubber boat to the cockpit, followed by the mechanic. Back in the cockpit I realized that we were already very low over the surface of the sea and I could assist the pilot by calling out the distance until we touched the water. Due to the lowered landing gear, the aircraft toppled over.

With the impact, I was thrown into the foremost part and, for a moment, was unconscious. Then, after having recovered, I noticed that we were under water, with water streaming through many openings. We slowly moved upwards and broke the surface, floating silently. We brought out our dinghy, inflated it as well as our lifebelts and boarded the rubber boat. At this moment we happened to see our wireless-operator move, indicating that he was still alive. So we hastened to bring the dinghy alongside and pulled our severely wounded crewman into it, at the same moment as the plane went down.

Now for the first time after our attack we were in a position to analyse our new situation. In view of the critical condition of our wireless operator, who was shot through an eye, the head, an arm and the chest, and since we were about 30kms off the British coast and could not hope to be rescued by German vessels, at least not during the night to come, we decided to use flares and markers in order to signal our position to a Short Sunderland flying boat that was circling a coastal convoy which we had encountered during air combat. About half an hour later a ship came in sight, the 'sub-chaser' Black Swan, *and rescued us. About 10 o'clock the next day we were transferred to another anti-submarine escort that brought us to Harwich, where we were put ashore at noon.'*

7

THREE AGAINST ONE
(NORTH YORKSHIRE MOORS,
11 AUGUST, 1940)

On 11 August a Ju.88A-1 (7A+KH; Werk Nu.2086) of 1/Aufklärungsgruppe 121 based at Stavanger, Norway, was ordered to carry out a high-altitude photo-reconnaissance of the Bomber Command aerodromes of Dishforth and Linton-on-Ouse. On that occasion its crew of *Feldwebel* Otto Höfft (pilot), *Feldwebel* Karl-Heinz Hacker (radio-operator) and *Oberleutnant* Hans Marzusch (observer), were joined by communications specialist *Leutnant* Heinrich Meier, whose job (presumably) was to gather radio intelligence. They took off in the late afternoon.

The flight across the North Sea would appear to have been uneventful, but as the raider approached the north-east coast fighter defences were alerted: at 6.25pm three Spitfires of Green Section, 'B' Flight, 41 Squadron, were ordered off from Catterick to patrol Teesmouth.

At 6.53pm the Ju.88 crossed in at 15,000ft over Whitby, where it was immediately identified by the town's Abbey Plain observation post as it passed over "at great speed in nearly direct line for Dishforth". The Spitfires

Men of the Abbey Plain observation post, Whitby, c.1945. Their post was in a field close to the abbey, which forms the backdrop of the picture.
Back row (L-R): *Jack Page; Norman Schofield; Frederick Askew; Joe Harrison (Head Observer); unknown; Harry Clarke; Frank Clarke.*
Front row (L-R): *unknown; Mr Ventrist; unknown; unknown; Alec Urmiston; Stan Wheetley; Percy Burnett; unknown.*
(photo: AR Askew)

were ordered to intercept, but a combination of distance and the fighters' dependence upon Observer Corps' tracking (relayed via Catterick Sector) meant that seventeen minutes would elapse before contact was established.

The Junkers was 18,000ft over Helmsley and on its way out when it was spotted by F/O John Boyle (Green 2). Some 30 seconds later it commenced a gradual diving turn to port and towards the safety of broken cloud 8,000ft below.

As Boyle swung in behind the intruder and began firing from 500yds, Otto Höfft steepened his dive but failed to take any other evasive action. Return fire was observed from the dorsal gun, but by the time Boyle had closed to 100yds and seconds before the Junkers reached the cloud, that defensive response had stopped.

F/O 'Wally' Wallens (Green 1) took up the chase as Boyle broke away. When cloud enveloped both pursued and pursuer he was a mere 40yds behind the raider but he reduced that to 25yds before firing, the sparks from his incendiaries allowing him to hold his aim in the misty conditions. Wallens' second burst was delivered from 50yds when the pair momentarily emerged into clear light; but before he lost his quarry on re-entering cloud, Wallens thought that the Junkers' port engine had stopped.

'Wally' Wallens (right) at the controls of an ASR Walrus. (RW Wallens)

Sgt 'Mitzi' Darling (Green 3) had remained above the cloud when the Junkers had first taken refuge but he had managed a couple of inconclusive squirts when Höfft emerged intermittently. However, he was more certain of the result when, after the Spitfires temporarily lost their quarry, he went below to find the Junkers just above the cloud base. He attacked from quarter to astern, using his sights to open fire and then bringing the easily visible cone of bullets on to the tail of the enemy aircraft. He emptied his guns before the enemy aircraft sank earthwards, descending very slowly in a shallow dive.

Home Guardsman Charles Rea, standing outside the Arncliffe Arms, Glaisdale, "heard the sound of gunfire and then saw the plane — Spitfires swooping around it — weazeling its way down and trailing smoke," as it struggled towards the coast. Twenty-six year old Tom Gallon was in Ugthorpe, attending a church service that was almost at an end when he heard the sound of aero-engines and machine-gun fire. In the company of almost the entire congregation he went

Sgt 'Mitzi' Darling. (Author's collection)

Junkers 88 7A+KH on Newton Moor, August, 1940. The white scarf mentioned by Tom Gallon's father hangs from the aerial above the cockpit. (Author's collection)

outside to witness the dog-fight as it progressed over Skelder Moor ("the Spits swooping and firing around him") and towards the sea.

Whether Höfft considered the possibility of an escape to seaward is a matter for conjecture. But with one engine already out, the prospect of a 400-mile trip across the ocean [assuming his (unlikely) escape from the Spitfires] on one engine would not be attractive. He did fly out over the water, however, but only for a short distance — just far enough to prompt the local observation post to wonder whether the Germans had dumped their camera offshore — before swinging back low over Hinderwell. At 7.30pm, and with the fighters still in attendance, Höfft made a wheels-up landing some 500yds east of the junction of the A.171 and B.1266.

Tom Gallon's father was on Newton Moor, close to where the crippled plane came to rest. He flung himself on the heather as Höfft eased the Junkers down and he did not budge until he saw one of the *Luftwaffe* crew hoist a mark of surrender (a white silk scarf) on the forward aerial. He was just getting up when Jack Soakell of High Farm, Borrowby — "A big riding man who had a good hunter or two to look after" — arrived on horseback. He was the first of a number of sightseers who flocked to the scene.

Tom Gallon was among them. When he arrived, Höfft, Hacker and

Marzusch were standing near their aircraft: the body of Meier, who had been killed in the attack, lay close by. He was 21 years old. Men from the nearby searchlight site on Sheffield Moor were among those already there. When they had seen the aircraft making its approach, they had taken a machine gun with them in anticipation of trouble, but, fortunately, it had not been needed. Now they had taken it upon themselves to keep the curious – and the souvenir hunters – at a respectable distance, pending the arrival of a more permanent guard.

The three survivors were soon removed from the site. Aided by Hinderwell Police Sergeant Welburn, Aaron Hart, an Ugthorpe butcher and Special Constable, used his butcher's van to transport them to Whitby police station, while Meier's body was removed to Thornaby. The plane remained on the moor for some days, a focus of local interest until its removal.

Perhaps understandably, the topic of conversation in the Ugthorpe 'local' that night centred around the crash. It was an occasion that offered one of the searchlight party the opportunity to boast that "the Germans wouldn't have walked off the moor if we had got there first: I would have shot the lot".

We shall never know whether such a statement owed more to bravado than to serious intent, but in any event Soakell may have taken exception to it, had

Aaron Hart (L) poses with his brother and their van in this 1930s photograph. (Mrs D. Fawkes)

he been there, for he had found the Germans to be "both amicable and courteous" when he had spoken to one who was fluent in English. Perhaps Tom Gallon would also have taken exception. One scene that impressed itself upon him fifty years ago, stays with him still:

> *"Three men were taken away. As they walked across the moor, one turned to look at the corpse – perhaps that of a friend – and started to cry like a baby."*

Postscript:

Höfft, Hacker and Marzusch were subsequently transported to a POW camp in Canada and returned to Germany after the cessation of hostilities. It is believed that they are still alive. Meier's body was buried in the RAF plot at Thornaby, which in those days was close to the perimeter of the aerodrome, and remained there until 1954, when it was transferred to Germany.

Of the Spitfire pilots, only Wally Wallens survived the war. He died in Stratford-on-Avon in February 1996. John Boyle was shot down and killed over Kent on 28 September, 1940; Edward ('Mitzi') Darling failed to return from a fighter sweep over France on 2 June, 1942.

The Observer Corps plot showing the flights of Ju.88 7A+KH and the three Spitfires of 41 Sqdn, Catterick, 11th August, 1940. The Ju.88 track commences over Whitby (square 33); that of the fighters starts over Redcar (square 04). (via Norman Spence)

8

'100 BANDITS...VECTOR 010'
(DURHAM COAST, 15 AUGUST, 1940)

The first time that Hans Kettling met Ted Shipman it was an occasion that offered little time for niceties, for Shipman was flying a Spitfire and Kettling was piloting a Messerschmitt 110. They met at 15,000 feet above the coast of County Durham on 15 August, 1940 − and each was trying to destroy the other.

It was the time when the Battle of Britain was at its height. Believing that available RAF fighter squadrons were heavily committed in the south, *Luftwaffe* bomber aircraft had launched a two-pronged attack from bases in Denmark and Norway against aerodromes in the north of England.

Fifty bombers of KG30 had been briefed to strike at Driffield aerodrome, East Yorkshire. At the same time, sixty-three Heinkel 111s of KG26 (Stavanger, Norway) had Dishforth and Linton-on-Ouse aerodromes as their primary targets, with Newcastle, Sunderland and Middlesbrough as their secondary aiming points.

The Heinkels, each carrying 3,000 pounds of bombs consisting of incendiaries and 500- and 250-kilo high explosives, were being escorted by twenty-one Messerschmitt 110 twin-engined fighters of I/ZG76. One of the Me.110s was flown by Kettling.

The Heinkels and their escort were detected by radar as they approached the north-east coast shortly after midday. Due to a serious error of navigation, they were some 70 miles north of their intended route, which should have ensured a landfall somewhere over the Durham coast.

When the error was realized and the raiders swung south in search of their targets they had no way of knowing that a number of seasoned fighter squadrons were 'resting' in the north and that they were already on alert.

Acklington-based Spitfires of 72 Squadron made the first contact, at 12.30pm off the Farne Islands. This was followed up by Hurricanes of Nos. 79 [Acklington], 605 [Drem] and 607 [Usworth] Squadrons.

These attacks cost the *Luftwaffe* at least seven aircraft and split the enemy force into two groups. One appears to have worked its way southwards along the coast towards the Tyne, constantly being harassed by fighters.

Over the land there was thick cumulus cloud, broken only occasionally by patches of blue. Thus the progress of the raiders was masked from ground-based observers, but many people on the Tyne and the Wear can

Hans Kettling with Uffz Fritz Stolper, his navigator/gunner, in Poland 1939. The aircraft is Me.110 M8+CH, which was shot down over Barnard Castle. (via Chris Goss)

still recall the ominously thunderous roar of aero-engines and the muted chatter of machine-gun fire as the Heinkels passed overhead.

Some of the bombers in that group jettisoned their loads over the Tyne shipyards and veered away out to sea while the remainder flew on towards Sunderland. The second group appears to have kept more to seaward: they were destined to meet 41 Squadron some ten miles off the Tyne.

Ted Shipman flew with 41 [Spitfire] Squadron, which had been heavily involved in the Battle from the outset. However, on 8 August the unit was temporarily 'rested' from the conflict that was raging in the south and was moved north to Catterick, a usually quiet sector – "convoy patrols interspersed with occasional interceptions of single intruders".

The first indication that something was afoot came at midday, when the entire squadron of thirteen Spitfires was 'brought to readiness'. At 12.40pm they were airborne, with instructions to 'patrol Hartlepool at 15,000 feet'.

The squadron lifted off from Catterick under the leadership of Flt/Lt Norman Ryder, but over Hartlepool it fell to P/O George Bennions to take over that role when it was realized that Ryder's radio was unserviceable.

Although a seasoned fighter pilot, George Bennions was not sure what to expect, but he does confess to being "thrilled and excited" when Ground Control ordered the interception of "100 Bandits on Vector 010". Following the course given and "climbing like hell to get up sun of them," the thirteen Spitfires sped northwards over the sea. George recalls:

> "I was thrilled and excited. Probably due to a desperate idea to get our own back after 29 July, 1940. Then we'd been at Manston [Kent] and had intercepted a similar number over Dover. But there had been about eighty Me.109 fighters and only twenty Ju.87 dive-bombers. As we attacked the bombers we were bounced by the 109s and lost five aircraft — almost half the squadron — in five minutes. But this was a different kettle of fish."

The cloud ceiling over the sea was at 5,000 feet, but the cumulus was not so thick; the breaks were more numerous. However, above that ceiling there was a haze that reduced visibility over longer distances. Thus the raiders were not spotted until they were a mere five miles away: an estimated fifty bombers grouped in fives in a mass arrowhead formation with fighter escort, their route being followed by shell bursts from the Tyne anti-aircraft defences. George remembers that:

> "The sky seemed full of big black dots and little black dots: the bombers in fives, the fighters in fours. The fighters were positioned some 500 yards behind and about 2,000 feet above, thus creating a dead man's land between the two formations where we might be caught between the rear guns of the Heinkels and the forward guns of the Messerschmitts."

As the Spitfires raced into the attack, Blue and Green Sections [six aircraft in total] were ordered to go for the escort while Bennions deployed the seven aircraft of Red and Yellow sections into echelon starboard for a beam attack on the bombers. Then they were among them and "in the mêlée all hell broke loose".

By this time they were over the Seaham Harbour area, where a number of Heinkels dropped bombs with tragic consequences, but individual combats would have the effect of scattering aircraft over a wider area reaching as far inland as Bishop Auckland and Barnard Castle.

Flying Officer Tony Lovell [Blue 1], an ex-Ampleforth College pupil and leader of Blue Section, went straight into the fray with the 110s. Choosing the last of a line of three, he opened with a concentrated burst of fire which caused his target to explode. Immediately, he fixed upon another which, after a burst of fire lasting eleven seconds, was to fall away, seemingly out of control. Sgt Howitt, his No.2, followed him and targeted the second of the trio; his short burst of fire raked the Messerschmitt from nose to tail before it plunged steeply towards the clouds some 13,000ft below, its progress marked by a trail of smoke.

Pilot Officer Ted Shipman [Green 1] ordered his section into echelon port to attack a group of 110s to the left of the formation. But before the Spitfires could get into range the Messerschmitts turned and flew straight towards them at an estimated closing speed of 400 mph. Shipman engaged the first in a head-on attack and managed a two-second burst before the enemy broke away to Shipman's port side "at very close range" and disappeared behind him. He next engaged another with an approach from the side, firing a number of shots without effect as his would-be victim took violent evasive action. Persisting with his attack, he closed to 200 yards astern and expended the rest of his ammunition. The enemy aircraft disappeared into cloud below, trailing smoke from the starboard engine and apparently out of control.

Pilot Officer 'Wally' Wallens [Green 3] escaped the head-on encounter with a half-roll that took him on to the tail of one of the escorts. He broke away and released a burst at another and sent it smoking into the clouds. Sgt Usmar [Green 2] spied a 110 crossing to attack Wallens. As the aircraft passed across his sights at 50 yards range, he gave it a short burst but was unable to observe the result because a bomber was flying straight at him. He fired and the Heinkel exploded with such force that it threw Usmar's machine upwards forty feet.

Yellow and Red Sections were primarily concerned with the bombers. After the first beam attack they ducked below the formation and climbed behind it. Norman Ryder [Yellow 2] went line astern on Bennions but found himself under attack from a Messerschmitt. He turned hard and managed to get astern of his pursuer. Three bursts of fire were enough to chip large pieces off the engine cowling before there "was a big explosion in the centre of the fuselage."

Meanwhile, Flying Officer John Mackenzie [Red 1] had chosen a 110 which was slightly starboard of the main formation. He opened fire at 200 yards. Smoke began pouring from the raider's starboard engine and continued to do so as the crippled aircraft dived into the protection of the cloud. Pilot Officer Eric Lock [Red 3] scored his first victory ever when his bullets found both engines of a 110 and sent it crashing into Seaham Harbour.

Pilot Officer George Bennions.

Following his initial foray against the bombers, George Bennions [Yellow 1] turned astern of the Heinkels. As he did so a 110 slid on to his tail. Jinking first to port then to starboard, he escaped his pursuer and found himself 300 yards astern of another. He fired and saw his shells striking home. The 110 immediately dived for the clouds

Hans Kettling's Me.110 at Streatlam, nr Barnard Castle. (Author's collection)

with Bennions in hot pursuit; he managed one last burst before his quarry disappeared.

When George emerged from the cloud he was over Barnard Castle; the Messerschmitt had crash-landed nearby. George was credited with the victory, but there is a suggestion that Ted Shipman may have initially disabled the 110 in an attack that shut down its starboard engine.

The pilot of the German fighter was *Oberleutnant* Hans Kettling:

"I heard Obergefreiter *Volk, my radio-operator and rear-gunner, fire his machine guns and on looking back I stared into the flaming guns of four Spitfires in splendid formation. The plane was hit — not severely, but the right-hand motor was dead, had lost its coolant and the oil temperature was rising rapidly. I had to shut off the ignition and bring the prop blades into the gliding position. I then tried to reach the protection of the bombers which*

were overhead, but without success. Over the radio I heard boys in the bombers talking about my aircraft so, as the Spitfires came in for the kill, I sent out my Mayday. This time the RAF fighters got the left-hand motor and knocked out the rear-gunner (who was wounded in the knee) and the front screen. The bullets missed my head by inches."

With both engines dead, Kettling crash-landed alongside Streatlam Camp, close to Bromielaw station, some three miles from Barnard Castle.

By that time (1.35pm), the attack on the north-east had virtually fizzled out and most of the raiders had fled: the few that remained scattered their bombs over County Durham, generally without strategic effect, before they too turned towards the sea. KG26 never found their original targets, the bomber bases at Dishforth and Linton-on-Ouse.

When it was over, the Catterick pilots were to claim one Heinkel and three Messerschmitts destroyed, four aircraft probably destroyed and five others damaged. It was a most impressive performance, achieved without loss and at a total cost of two bullet holes in the wing of one Spitfire.

Accounts of the cost of the raid to the *Luftwaffe* do vary, but it may be that they lost fifteen aircraft over the coastal areas of Northumberland and Durham on 15 August, 1940: the first − and the last − large-scale daylight raid on the north had been routed. From that time on, large-scale raids on the area would be launched under the cover of darkness.

In the post-war years many former 'enemies' who confronted each other over Britain during the last war have re-established contact on a more peaceful footing. Among those ex-fliers are to be found Hans Kettling and Ted Shipman, who have become firm friends who share holidays together. Although Ted now lives in the Midlands and Kettling in Germany, occasionally they can be seen tramping the fields near Bromielaw station, map in hand and with an eye to the sky.

George Bennions lives locally: he has never met Hans Kettling.

EYE-WITNESS
The War
Air Raid − 15 August, 1940

On Thursday morning Audrey and I had the most exciting yet frightening adventure of our lives. We had taken the dogs for a walk beside the Foxhunters Inn, Monkseaton, through the fields, and we were just climbing the trees there, when we heard the air raid siren. (It was 12.50pm.) What a shock we got; we could hardly believe it was real. We called the dogs and we all ran like mad, even Pam (my lazy Sealyham) ran!

We only ran a little way when we thought, supposing the German planes

EXCITABLE FOLK
Smiling Through By LEE

"Quite, Madam, but I doubt very much if they can hear
you."

come over and machine-gun us — so we dived into a hedge and cuddled together.

A little later, the noise started. It was awful! The guns (anti-aircraft) made an awful noise and the drone of the planes was terrible. We saw a German plane dash through the balloon barrage, the guns firing at it. We couldn't see too much because we were under the trees, but the aeroplanes made an awful noise and the machine-gunning was terrific. A dog-fight was going on.

For a long time we lay cuddled together with cotton wool in our ears and the dog leashes between our teeth (to stop the dogs running away). Then the noise stopped and we saw five fighter planes fly out towards the sea. British, I think. A few minutes later, when these five planes had gone, a huge German plane (Junkers, I think) came swooping out of the clouds and made for the sea.

Another little English fighter (Spitfire or Hurricane, I think) dashed after it, and it looked small compared to the huge German bomber. Then the big German plane dashed off into the clouds after the anti-aircraft guns fired at it.

A few seconds later we saw a little plane which was being fired at — then it too disappeared.

All became very quiet and I gave Audrey and myself a bit of chewing gum. After sitting there a little longer, the 'All Clear' went.

I don't think I ever felt so thankful in all my life. We dashed for my home (Beverley Park) where Mum was so glad to see us. She had been very worried.

Audrey rang up her house to say she was safe, then she went home. I had dinner, and related my adventures to Mummy.

The 'All Clear' had sounded at 2.20pm. It was exciting yet frightening in a way, because Audrey and I have never been out alone a fairly good way from home before in an air raid.

P.S. The dogs were very good.

Extract from the diary of Norah Welch (née Parker), now of Tynemouth, who was 10 years old in 1940.

9

FATAL INTERCEPTION
(WHITBY, 7 SEPTEMBER, 1940)

In September, 1940, Alan Deere was a Flight Lieutenant with 54 (Spitfire) Squadron. Deere served with great distinction both during the Battle of Britain and after it. In continuous action from the outbreak of war until 1943, his official 'score' was: twenty-two enemy aircraft destroyed; ten probables; eighteen damaged. In September 1940 the squadron was 'rested' from the Battle which was raging in the south and was posted to Catterick, where it was to operate as a temporary training squadron until it returned to the south of England in February, 1941.

Deere recalls that:

"We were soon into the relaxed routine of this quiet sector, but, as a result of the German attack on the north-east on 15 August, the squadron was required to keep one flight at readiness at the satellite airfield at Greatham, on the coast near West Hartlepool. It was a boring business having to spend the whole day at Greatham with, as it were, only a telephone for company and one which, unlike its counterpart at Rochford, very rarely rang.

I had an odd experience during one of the few scrambles from Greatham. I intercepted a Junkers 88 near Whitby but before I could fire a shot, and after he had dropped his bomb, the pilot sought the safety of the clouds and headed off east out to sea. There was absolutely no point in trying to ferret him out of the cloud, so I orbited in the vicinity awaiting orders from Control. My Number 2, a Polish pilot, who was seeing his first German aircraft since his arrival in England, had tasted blood and could not be restrained. He shot into the cloud after the Hun, despite my orders to the contrary, and was never seen or heard of again.

A plot was followed from the position where they both had entered the cloud until the track was lost about forty miles off the coast. I suspect that the Pole just flew on, further and further out to sea and discovered too late that he was short of petrol and out of R/T range. Perhaps he got the Junkers in the end, but I doubt it. Like many similar incidents during the war, his disappearance remains a mystery."

[Alan C. Deere: Nine Lives, Hodder & Stoughton, 1959]

The Pole was Pilot Officer W. Krepski, who had joined the squadron only

Flight Lieutenant Alan Deere. (Author's collection)

sixteen days earlier. He was officially listed as having failed to return from an operational sortie over the Flamborough area at 2.30pm on 7 September, 1940. It was believed that he had lost his bearings due to R/T failure and had crashed into the sea.

Luftwaffe records of losses for the same date list a Junkers 88 of II/KG54 as having failed to return from operations over England and that its exact fate was unknown. It was presumed that its crew were dead and that the aircraft had been lost.

Perhaps Deere was wrong: perhaps Krepski *did* get the Junkers in the end? Alan Deere died in September 1995.

10

THE NIGHT OF THE 'BOMBER'S MOON'. (MIDDLESBROUGH, 13 OCTOBER, 1940)

At 7.55pm on Sunday, 13 October, 1940, a single German aircraft dropped four 250lb high-explosives on the Marsh Road area of Middlesbrough and caused severe damage to properties in Benjamin Street, Hatherley Street, Nixon Street, Hartington Street, Marsh Road, Argyle Street, Farrer Street and Cannon Street. Although the scale of destruction would be surpassed at a later date, the number of casualties inflicted on that autumn evening was among the highest that the town's population would suffer in any air raid during the Second World War.

Earlier in the day Ethel Gaunt and a number of her colleagues had settled around a table at the Lord Street First Aid Post, off Cannon Street, for a belated celebration of her birthday of three days earlier: there should have been fourteen at the party, but one could not make it. For the superstitious, two thirteens together was perhaps tempting Providence — and at least one of those present commented upon the coincidence. That particular observation was laughed off, but within hours the siren was wailing to herald the attack in which Ethel, a St John Ambulance First Aider (ARP) attached to the Lord Street Post, would see her worst casualties of the war in what became known as the 'Marsh Road incident'.

It was a night of the 'bomber's moon', an evening of brilliant moonlight which, for a high-flying raider, at least, illuminated the town as if it were daytime. Perhaps it was those conditions which partly accounted for the large numbers of people who were walking about the streets when the bombs fell; that, perhaps, and the fact that nineteen minutes elapsed between the sounding of the 'Alert' and the crump of the first explosion. Certainly it seemed that many citizens had not taken to the shelters, but even for those who had, the evening's events would show that *no* place was entirely safe during an air raid and that Chance had a role to play.

Among those out walking that evening was 14-year-old Albert Farrow, who was strolling down Beaufort Street, close to the North Riding Infirmary, with his cousin. They had chosen to ignore the warning, "but some minutes later there was a terrific bang and we flew into the nearest shelter feeling petrified".

Fifteen-year-old Ernie Reynolds could not ignore the siren: for him it was a call to duty. He was a Messenger at the Holy Cross First Aid Post in

Rescue and Demolition Parties begin clearance work at 53 Benjamin Street.
(Cleveland County Archives)

Cannon Street and he had gone straight there. However, when the bombs started to fall he shared common ground with the two boys in Beaufort Street because "the bombs shrieked down so loudly that we all thought that they were meant for us".

The first bomb fell on railway premises near the Metz Bridge, North Road, where it demolished the LNER Goods' Master's office and two nearby signal posts. North Road was partly blocked by debris and there was superficial damage — mainly shattered windows — to Dorman, Long Britannia Works, Richard Hill's Wire Works and a warehouse owned by Younger's Brewery. Unlike the three that followed, the first high-explosive caused no casualties.

The second exploded between two cast-iron shelters at the junction of Farrer Street and Marsh Road. Its lethal power blew out the ends of both shelters, demolished seven houses in Marsh Road, caused irreparable damage to houses in adjacent streets and made a crater 25ft in diameter and 12ft deep.

The third struck one end of a cast-iron shelter at the junction of Benjamin Street and Hatherley Street. It made only a small crater but the blast wiped out eight houses in Hatherley Street and caused considerable damage to domestic property in the vicinity.

The final bomb landed midway between the back of Benjamin Street and Farrer Street, again causing large-scale destruction to housing.

In the seconds that it took for those explosives to blast their way through the community fifteen houses were demolished, thirty-seven were rendered so dangerous that they would have to be pulled down, thirty-eight were reduced to a state so unsafe that they would have to be evacuated, and a further 100 were badly damaged. In addition, 300 properties were affected to a lesser degree.

For the superstitious, perhaps two thirteens together *had* tempted Providence. And for those searching for 'signs' in coincidences perhaps the films showing at the town's Scala cinema in Newport Road that week — *Remember the Night* and *Everything Happens at Night* — were not without significance.

Fate dealt some cruel blows on 13 October, 1940, and a number of families were destined to experience the sadness of bereavement; but to others Fate was particularly kind and with the passing of time they would find themselves speculating on the role played by Chance.

Prior to the attack, ARP Warden Mrs Collins was attending chapel in Cannon Street. When the 'Alert' sounded she returned to her Hartington Street home to prepare for duty. *Unusually*, she left her home via the *back* door. Had she gone her usual way, the chances are that she would have stopped to talk to Bill Butterwick, who lived at No. 9 and who was often to be found standing at the street corner. Butterwick's crippled daughter, Bella,

"...families gleaned what possession they could from the debris and heaped them into meagre piles..." Hartington Street, October, 1940. (Cleveland County Archives)

was also attending chapel and had taken her small child with her; when the Alarm sounded he was concerned for their safety and shortly before the bombs plummeted earthwards he was once again at the corner, anxiously awaiting their return. Seconds after Mrs Collins left by the back entrance, the second bomb struck. Butterwick was killed instantly; Mrs Collins was not even scratched. Nor were his daughter and grandchild for they had reached a place of safety just before the bombs fell.

Mrs Bacon and her six children *thought* they were in a safe place when the attack got underway, for they were crouching in the cast-iron shelter at the junction of Benjamin Street and Hatherley Street. When the bomb that was to explode close by screamed earthwards, the mother threw herself over three of her family in an effort to protect them. Fate was kind: they were almost buried in the shambles that remained after the explosion, but they survived. Her 10-year-old son, Tommy, was able to crawl out unaided and unscathed, yet the boy and girl who had been sitting on either side of him were killed. An ARP worker and his family of four had a similarly remarkable escape when the second bomb landed close to *their* shelter. The entire group was catapulted out of one end but they escaped with scratches; the same blast killed other occupants.

There were others who had cause to be grateful: an ARP worker who was 'phoning from the local rescue station when the raid occurred was blown through a window and escaped with a cut knee; a customer in a pub on the fringe of the area was in the process of lifting his glass to his lips when shock waves wrenched it from his hand but left him untouched; Mrs M. Ryan, a refugee from the London blitz, was washing herself alongside the window in her sister's kitchen when the blast lifted her off her feet, threw her across the room and dashed her against a table, where she sustained some bruising but no serious injury.

However, some were less fortunate: the two young men who were to report for call-up the next day and who were killed as they stood talking in the street; Daisy Sherwood, of 69 Hatherley Street, who left her home with a large jug in her hand merely seconds before the first bomb fell and who was *en route* to the off-licence but who never completed her journey; the anonymous man who usually stayed at home during raids but who, having decided that a public shelter might be safer, was scythed down as he made his way there. There were also others, but their deaths were less public: they lay under the pounded remnants of what had once been called 'home'.

Corporal Farrow, Home Guard, was among the first would-be rescuers to arrive at the corner of Benjamin Street and Hatherley Street, where the scene was one of great devastation. Scores of houses had met the full effect of the blast: some had collapsed totally, while others had been divested of walls, ceilings, slates and windows, the mounds of shattered masonry entombing casualties, blocking thoroughfares and throwing down the first real challenge of the war to the town's rescue services. A thin film of soot, ejected from domestic chimneys by the shock waves, covered everything and everyone; there was the faint smell of smoke from the first of thirty-one fires caused by hot cinders sprayed from domestic grates by blast. Sad though the scene was, Farrow saw more poignant reminders of War's cruelty: the corpse of a young soldier at the corner of Hatherley Street and, in a wrecked shelter nearby, a number of people sitting lifeless yet without apparent injury.

He was soon joined by the town's mayor, Cllr Sir William Crosthwaite, and together they set about tending to casualties, the mayor tearing his tailor-made silk shirt into makeshift bandages which he and Farrow then used to treat some of the injured.

Fortunately, there was a Rescue Party depot in the area and so *organized* rescue was soon underway, but the task was not easy. Apart from the disruption of communications, workers found that it was sometimes necessary to use 20-ton jacks and shoring in order to clear ways through to victims trapped within their crumbled homes. Some victims had already been reached before the First Aid parties arrived and the lack of stretchers, which were the latter's responsibility, badly hampered the rescuers in the initial stages. However, it was already too late for some, including the man whom rescuers had to dig out from a partially collapsed structure and who had clearly been using his own body to protect the baby whose fragile form lay under him. Both were dead.

Working with the aid of spotlights and hand-lamps, rescuers toiled through most of the night to reach those in need and those beyond help. The dead and the seriously injured were taken directly to the North Riding Infirmary, while local First Aid stations dealt with less serious cases. Immediately after the raid, Hugh Bell School was opened as a temporary Emergency Feeding Centre and during the following three days a maximum of 311 homeless persons were accommodated and fed until alternative housing could be arranged.

By the following morning, the real 'slogging' by clearance squads had given the streets a tidier appearance, but it would take some time for the job to be completed. In some streets, groups of sad-eyed bystanders watched wistfully as squads continued to remove the rubble of 'home'; in others, families gleaned what possessions they could from the debris and heaped them into meagre piles before joining the streams of other victims who passed to and fro, pushing prams or hand-carts piled with what little they had managed to salvage.

The mayor spent much of the night tending victims, visiting casualties in hospital and talking to families in the Emergency Feeding Centre. What he saw and heard touched him deeply. On 14 October he launched his appeal for the establishment of the Middlesbrough Emergency Relief Fund, from which people in distressed circumstances could receive grants in cash or in

The remnants of 168 Marsh Road, the home of 58-year-old Mary Emmerson who suffered fatal injuries and died later in North Riding Infirmary. (Cleveland County Archives)

kind when there were no central or local government grants available, or to supplement such grants if they were found to be inadequate. He appealed for a public subscription to create a fund of £10,000, he himself making the first donation (of £1,000). Such was the generosity of the townsfolk that it took just eighteen days to reach the target, while gifts of furniture were on such a scale that special premises had to be acquired to store all that was donated.

When a final reckoning could be made it was clear that the *material* cost of the attack had been high. Time would ensure that it was met. However, the human cost was far higher: twenty dead, of whom four died after admission to hospital; thirty-two seriously injured and seventy-two with minor injuries. In this regard, there was no guarantee that Time would discharge the hurt.

Subsequently, Mrs Bacon would philosophize that "When you get over the shock of a first bombing you don't feel so badly about any others," while Mrs Ryan would point out that, "This was only a flea-bite compared with what London has had." Flea-bite or not, many would take a long time to come to terms with their experiences.

There were those who voiced the view that, "This isn't warfare, it's wholesale murder." But War always was — and no doubt always will be. However, there is evidence to suggest that the casualties of that night were the consequences of an accident. Middlesbrough's Chief Constable, Mr A. E. Edwards, was quick to point out in his report to the Regional Police Staff Officer, No.1 (Northern) Region, Newcastle, that the location of the damage was very near to the Britannia Works of Dorman, Long, and a number of other Works, the railway marshalling yards and the town's gasometers. Thus, whilst it is not known what the raider's objective was, in the Chief Constable's view the bomber's aim was "not very inaccurate in relation to the location of the many essential Works and Services". The bombs had fallen short and civilians had paid the price. It was a precedent that would be followed on a number of subsequent occasions in the town's history during those dark days, but never to the extent that other centres were to suffer.

The raider did achieve a limited success, however. Blast damage affected a number of windows at Richard Hill's Wire Works and for a short time output had to be restricted due to the emission of light at night. In retrospect, it seems to have been a terrible price to pay for the short-term ruination of the black-out precautions.

EYE-WITNESS
"On Sunday night, 13 October, 1940, the sirens sounded while a neighbour was shaving. Man-like, he decided to finish it. Suddenly there was a bang; a flash. The mirror disappeared and the window-frame came over his head.
'Oh, Katie, come quick,' he shouted. 'I've gone and cut my head off through the Germans!' "

Mrs M. McDermott, resident of the Marsh Road area, 1940.

EYE-WITNESS

"On Sunday, 13 October, 1940, I was sent to the Marsh Road incident, where I came across an old woman and two small children, all in bad condition. I could not make up my mind which one needed attention most. On seeing my hesitation, the woman said: 'See to the children first,' which I did. She would not let me dress her wound but insisted on my taking the children to the Lord Street Post first. So I gave her a dressing to hold on her wound.

Hurrying back after delivering the children into the doctor's hands, I asked her the reason for her action. With tear-dimmed eyes she said quietly: 'I have lived my life: theirs lies ahead.'

Later she died. The babies recovered."

Miss E. Dawson, resident at CDR Hostel, Great Ayton, 1940.

EYE-WITNESS

"I was a member of the 24th (Middlesbrough) Scout Group. In 1939 I joined the ARP Messenger Service after our scout-master, Mr Gosnay, asked for volunteers. I was given a battle-dress uniform and a gas-mask and I was attached to the Middlesbrough Town Hall HQ Post. Whenever the siren sounded I was expected to report to the Town Hall, where I would make tea or take messages and generally help out where possible. Sometimes I would go out with a policeman during a raid so that I could deliver messages for him, should that be necessary.

On 13 October I was on my way down Newport Road to the Town Hall when the bombs fell. The blast flung me and my bike through Smart's shop window but I suffered only slight cuts so I went down to the bombed area, where I reported to the person in charge. After a while I got sick of hanging around doing nothing so I started helping out — pulling out injured, that kind of thing.

Later, when I was looking around to help, I heard moaning so I started looking around for the source. I found a young lady lying on the pavement, near a wall. She was dirty, bleeding and in some difficulty. I spat on my handkerchief and started to clean her up. She was mumbling and I eventually realized that she was trying to tell me that her baby was on the way! I went in search of an ambulance-man, told him what was happening and then went back to stay with her until help came. The baby was born while we were waiting. I helped her to wrap it in a blanket and then stayed with her until the ambulance finally arrived.

I remember that there were a lot of people wandering about, dazed. A hall was opened up in Cannon Street and tea and soup and food were served to people. I spent three days there helping out."

Dennis Chambers, resident of Bruce Avenue, Whinney Banks, October, 1940.

EYE-WITNESS

"I was a messenger boy at the Holy Cross First Aid Post in Cannon Street. The ambulances we had were delivery vans and furniture vans and the like. They arrived at the Holy Cross in the evening after the working day was over and we screwed stretchers on to the floorboards. They stood in the street all night and the drivers collected them the next morning after the stretchers had been removed, thus reverting their role to delivery vans.

When the casualties began to arrive on 13 October it became somewhat chaotic because a lot of casualties were brought in by relatives or friends, all demanding instant attention for them.

It was the first time I had seen victims of bombing and I was amazed that they were all black. It seems that when houses are bombed they get severely shaken and all the soot comes down the chimneys and covers everything and everyone in the vicinity.

One man hopped in and rested his hand on my shoulder, nearly collapsing me. I got him to hop to a chair and rolled up his trouser leg. He had a jagged metal splinter, about six inches long, in the centre of his knee — but there was very little blood."

Mr E. Reynolds, resident at 42 Dale Street, Middlesbrough, 1940.

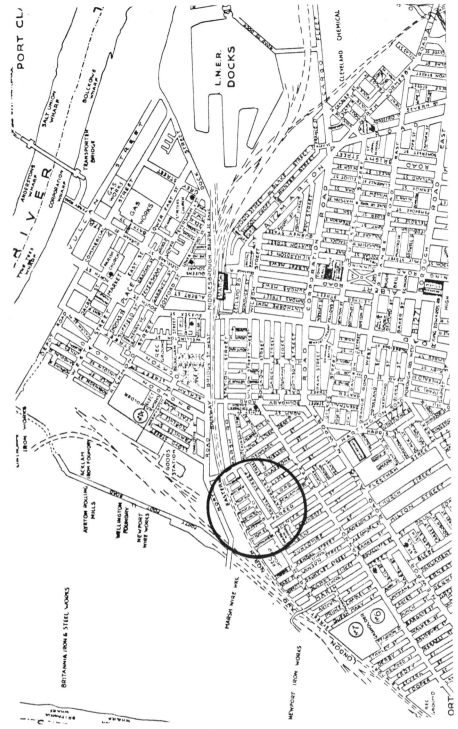

13 October 1940: The Marsh Road Incident.

11

INCIDENT AT DUGGLEBY
(YORKSHIRE WOLDS, 27 OCTOBER, 1940)

Jack Clarke had many visitors during the fifty or so years that he farmed Manor Farm, Duggleby, near Malton, but perhaps the ones he remembers most vividly were four strangers who dropped in one evening in late autumn 1940.

In the late afternoon and early evening of Sunday, 27 October, 1940, German aircraft launched a series of attacks against aerodromes in East Anglia, Lancashire and Yorkshire. A number of those airfields were in the Malton area: Linton-on-Ouse, Catfoss, Leconfield and Driffield.

One of the three aircraft assigned to attack Driffield was a Junkers Ju.88 twin-engined bomber [5J+ER] of 7/*KG4* based at Amsterdam/Schiphol; its crew were *Oberleutnant* Friedrich Podbielski and *Unteroffiziers* Hans Heier, Karl von Kidrowski and Osker Piontek.

The three raiders delivered their low-level attack at 6.00pm, when a number of small-calibre bombs were dropped and the drome buildings were machine-gunned: no casualties resulted and practically no damage was done. However, one bomb exploded on the Kellythorpe road, alongside the airfield, making a crater some twenty feet deep and some thirty feet across and rupturing a six-inch water main.

Such damage was almost inconsequential, but the effect of return fire from ground defences was to prove disastrous for Podbielski and his crew.

Seventy-year-old Matt Young now lives in quiet retirement in Stockton-on-Tees, but in October, 1940, he was a Lewis Gunner with 'D' Section, 411 Battery, 54 Searchlight Regt. RA (TA). *His* searchlight was located in the fields of Fimber Field Farm, in a hollow alongside the A.166 and midway between the villages of Fridaythorpe and Wetwang, and it was his task to defend it in the event of air attack.

On a clear day the men at Fimber could see the aerodrome at Driffield from their raised position on the Wolds, but in the early evening of 27 October, 1940, the airfield was masked by haze.

Matt remembers:

"Sergeant Frazer had just arrived with the ration waggon. He was on site when we heard the bombs dropping at Driffield aerodrome. We couldn't see anything because of the haze, but I immediately went to the gun position

Matt Young, Lewis gunner, 1940. (M. Young)

and we got orders from HQ at Huttons Ambo that we could engage the enemy — but at first we couldn't see anything."

Then two Ju.88s gradually emerged from the haze. They were in loose formation and they were not flying very high. The bombers "flew in almost a straight line from Driffield; straight up the hillside," towards the searchlight position. As they drew near, Matt felt the urge to shoot but Frazer refused permission on the grounds that "They might fire back!" and made Matt wait for a safer opportunity.

"Just before they reached us, they started to bank to starboard, as if making for the coast. When they were about halfway round he let me fire.
I set the gun going, followed my tracers and directed the full pan of 47 rounds into the port engine of the one nearest me. They got round with their tails towards us and I put on another pan and fired again, but I don't know if it did any good. They didn't fire back, anyway."

As the bombers disappeared eastwards into the haze, Matt began to believe that he had caused no damage for both seemed to be getting safely away. However, "people at Fridaythorpe who had been watching all the time said that after I had finished firing and the planes were going back towards the coast the one I'd hit veered off."

In fact, 5J+ER had suffered critical damage: at least one member of the crew was wounded, the port engine was out and the starboard engine was impaired.

As the Ju.88 left the target area, its crew must have realized that a safe return to base would be accomplished only with difficulty and a good measure of luck. In an effort to maximise the latter, Podbielski instructed his men to jettison any equipment that could be manhandled out of the aircraft.

Shortly after 6.00pm, Jack Clarke was busy shutting up the poultry huts in his fields at Manor Farm, Duggleby, [nr Malton], when he heard the "laboured" sounds of an aero-engine approaching from the direction of North Grimston. Seconds later, the crippled bomber barely crested "Duggleby Plum", the rising land to the north of the village, before settling even lower. As it lurched towards Jack and the farm buildings some two hundred yards behind him, its flight path was marked by the debris of equipment discarded by the crew in an effort to lighten the load and gain more lift. But it was to no avail: the necessary power was lacking and the plane was sinking even nearer to the ground.

When it staggered over Jack Clarke, "It was very very low," no more than thirty feet above the ground. He could see that a crash was inevitable, but whether the raider was to come to earth on the farm buildings or on the open land beyond was a matter over which he had no control.

Ju88 (5J+ER) of 7/KG4 under guard at Duggleby, October 1940. (Northern Echo)

Podbielski might well have felt the same and could have been bracing himself for the worst, but Fate was kind: the Junkers skimmed over Clarke's Dutch barn, narrowly missed the chimney pots of a house behind the farm, bellied into the field that rises to the ancient barrow of "Duggleby Howe" and gouged its way to the top of the rise before coming to rest alongside the hedge that runs eastwards from the Howe. Jack set off in pursuit, but he soon found that he was not alone.

"Six of us scrambled up the hill towards it: myself, 'Josh' Jeffles, Bill Jeffles, Harold Hodgson, Ben Midgeley and John Gray. As we approached the plane three of the crew started walking towards us, hands raised in surrender. When we got within twenty yards of them, one started to gesture with his hands — repeatedly raising them to elbow level. We stopped. He persisted in doing this and after a few moments he set off back towards the plane.

A number of us knew of the practice of crashed crews destroying their aircraft to prevent them falling into enemy hands — and so when one of the Jeffles boys shouted, 'Hey up, he's going to blow her up!' there was a mad scramble back down the hill. Until then, I had thought that I could run fast, but I was the last one down to the bottom."

However, there was no explosion. And when the would-be helpers realized that it was not the crew's intention to 'fire' their aircraft, they cautiously returned. It was then that they realized the significance of the earlier gesture:

A soldier of the Manchester Regiment examines the Gruppen badge of Ju.88 (5J+ER) of 7/KG4 that crashed at Duggleby, nr Malton, on 27 October, 1940, after being struck by ground-fire during an attack on Driffield aerodrome. (Northern Echo)

a fourth crewman [OskerPiontek] was pinned under the tail and was obviously badly injured; his colleague had been asking for help.

Whether Piontek had panicked and had jumped out as the plane had skidded across the field or had been thrown out on impact was not clear, but it did "seem the human thing to help free him," and in a spontaneous demonstration of War's ironies friend and foe joined together to lift the tail unit and help a fellow human-being.

They used an overcoat as a makeshift stretcher and carried the injured man to Clarke's farm, where they placed him on the kitchen table. While Mrs Clarke got a pillow on which to rest Piontek's head, his friends removed his boots and his gloves and tried to make him comfortable as best they could, but Piontek "was as good as dead even then. There was not a sound from him. He was very badly injured and had a gaping hole in his left side, presumably where the plane had been resting on him". Though they might try, in reality there was little that they could do but wait for the arrival of the military and, hopefully, professional help.

When members of the locally-billeted Manchester Regiment arrived on the scene shortly afterwards they came with fixed bayonets and took a "very military stance," forcing the crew to strip to the waist to ensure that they concealed no weapons. It was a gesture that some of those present felt to be

This 1943 photograph shows five of the Kirby Grindalythe Home Guard who guarded the Duggleby Ju.88 on the first night. Back row (L to R): *Thomas Freer, Lesley Morrison, Harry Lightfoot.*
Front row (L to R): *David Silborne (Lt.), Walter Lightfoot.* (W. Lightfoot)

unnecessary and "rather ridiculous, for the crew were totally harmless...none of them gave any trouble."

Podbielski was subsequently taken to York, the rest to Driffield, where Osker Piontek died from his injuries on 15 November 1940. He is buried in the German war cemetery (*Deutschen Soldatenfriedhof*), Cannock Chase, Staffordshire.

During those wartime days, most people were souvenir-hunters. It seemed that everyone, irrespective of age, wanted a piece of a crashed German aircraft: a memento of what seemed at the time, anyway, a momentous occasion. Jack Clarke was no exception.

He recalls being very impressed by the quality of the clothing worn by the fliers, so when the Manchesters left behind Piontek's knee-length fur-lined flying boots and black kid-gloves, Jack resolved "to take care of them'. The boots were not in his charge for long, however. A couple of visits by Sgt Huddleston of the Driffield Constabulary, who confessed to being "totally unable to understand why this fellow was flying in bare feet," was enough to ensure that the boots were 'found' and duly handed over. The gloves, however, were never mentioned by Sgt Huddlestone: they served their new owner for many years after the war had ended.

Postscript:

Although there seems little doubt that Matt Young was responsible for shooting down the Junkers, it was some three days before he was allowed to visit the wreck. After he had submitted his report he was confined to the Fimber site until he had been questioned by Service 'Big-wigs.' It seems that a detachment of the 38th Light AA Regt, employed in the defence of Driffield aerodrome, had also claimed the Junkers as theirs and so there had to be an enquiry. "Finally, it was decided that I had to share it with the 38th, but I don't know why."

411 Battery subsequently received a letter of congratulations from Command HQ and Matt was later informed that they would have liked to have seen him Mentioned in Despatches. However, it was not to be.

Uffz Oskar Piontek was a crew member of a Ju. 88 [5J+ER] of 7/KG4 which crashed at Duggleby, nr Malton, on 27 October 1940. He died from his injuries on 15 November 1940 and now lies in the German War Cemetery (Deutschen Soldatenfriedhof) Cannock Chase, Staffs. He shares a grave with Feldw. Willi Meyer, crew member of a Fw 200 [F8+EH] of 1/KG40 which was shot down by AA fire on 19 July 1940 while mine-laying between Hartlepool and Crimdon Dean. (Author)

EYE-WITNESS

Jim Penrose, now of Richmond, North Yorks, had a narrow escape on 27 October, 1940. He was then a Water Board superintendent living at the Driffield RDC pumping station in Southburn Lane, Hutton Cranswick.

The raider passed low over his premises seconds before Jim went to chain up his dog at its kennel alongside the garage. He recalls that:

"As I bent down by the kennel to fasten the chain I heard a rat-tat-tat. I shot round behind the garage on my tummy and stayed there a minute or two until he was completely out of sight. When I came back I noticed a row of holes across the front of the kennel. There was a machine-gun bullet sticking half-way out of one of them. I dug it out with my pen-knife. And I still have it."

Military personnel examine the wreckage of a Ju.88A-1 which had crashed on the North Yorkshire Moors the previous evening, 2 November, 1940. The aircraft, coded 4D+TS (*Werk Nu.7089*), belonged to 8/KG30 and was based at Eindhoven (Holland). It was *en route* to attack the aerodrome at Linton-on-Ouse when it encountered fog and struck the steep hillside at Glaisdale Head, nr Whitby. The crew — *Feldwebel* Wilhelm Wowereit; *Oberfeldwebel* Hans Schulte-Mater; *Unteroffizier* Alfred Rodermond; *Unteroffizier* Gerhard Pohling — were killed in the crash and now lie in the Royal Air Force plot at the Acklam Road cemetery, Thornaby-on-Tees. (E. Baxter/*Evening Gazette*)

12

A JU.88 CRASHES
(ESTON HILLS, CLEVELAND,
30 MARCH, 1941)

To the casual observer walking along the southern edge of the Eston Hills, the chance discovery of a meagre accumulation of twisted fragments of aluminium, pieces of charred rubber, and a sizable remnant of scorched leather would probably not warrant a second glance. And yet those artefacts are as much a part of Cleveland's history as those more celebrated examples which are to be found in any museum in the locality. Those oddments are nearly all that remains to remind us of a brief air battle that was fought in the skies over Cleveland on the afternoon of Sunday, 30 March, 1941, when a German bomber was shot down over Barnaby Moor.

On that day, Home Guardsman Alf Kirby was receiving practice in the firing of the Browning machine gun on the range at the foot of Eston Hills and close to Flatts Lane when he heard the distant wail of sirens. Shortly afterwards he saw a pair of Spitfires following the Tees towards the coast before they climbed to 2,500 feet and disappeared into the 6/10 cloud which hung over the area.

The two Spitfires were flown by Flt/Lt Tony Lovell and P/O Archie Winskill, both of 'B' Flight, 41 Squadron, Catterick. They had taken off from their base at 2.50pm with orders to patrol Seaham Harbour. An incoming raider had been plotted approaching the English coast north of Sunderland: if it swung south Lovell and Winskill would be well placed to attempt interception.

The raider was a Junkers Ju.88 (4U+GH) of 1/Aufklärungsgruppe 123 and was crewed by *Leutnant* Wolfgang Schlott (pilot), *Leutnant* Otto Meingold (observer), *Feldwebel* Wilhelm Schmigale (radio-operator) and *Unteroffizier* Hans Steigerwald (gunner). They were on a photo-reconnaissance sortie to Manchester, but when they banked left and began to fly parallel to the Durham coast they were also on what would prove to be a collision course with the fighters.

While daylight incursions over the British coast were always dangerous — and the raiders would have been well aware of the risks — perhaps on that occasion the crew felt reasonably safe at their altitude of 25,000 feet. With the cloud layer 18,000 feet below providing a backcloth of brilliant white against which any interceptors might be easily spotted, and with their aircraft's

Flt/Lt Tony Lovell (centre) with fellow pilots of 41 (Spitfire) Squadron, Catterick, 1940. (N. Ryder)

light blue undersides blending in totally with the sky above, the combination of height and camouflage had reduced the risk of attack to a minimum.

The raider's alteration of course to the south was noted by Ground Control and at 2.58pm, when Lovell and Winskill were approaching the Tees estuary, they were ordered to intercept.

They climbed through 7,000 feet of cloud and emerged into clear blue sky, but they could not see the Junkers. Five minutes later, and at 17,000 feet, they still could not see the intruder, but they spotted a vapour trail some 7,000 feet above, to the left of their position and moving in the opposite direction. Lovell and Winskill climbed "flat out in a climbing turn and followed the trail, which hid us very effectively".

So successful was *that* camouflage that the Spitfires were able to close to within 250 yards of their target before Lovell elected to execute the attack with a three-second burst of gunfire which shot away pieces of the Ju.88 before it dived away steeply towards cloud with the fighters in close pursuit.

When the trio emerged from the cloud, they were over Redcar. Observers in that town might well have expected the Junkers to crash there, but pilot Wolfgang Schlott managed to pull out and the raider skimmed low over the roof-tops, its attackers close behind and "pumping terrific bursts of gunfire into the German aircraft".

Although obviously crippled and with no chance of escape, the Junkers twisted and writhed its way over East Cleveland. When it approached Smith's Dockyard, employee Jim Cox noticed that it was flying "fairly high but not very high," and that it was being harassed by two fighters "one alongside while the other swooped on top". Neil Jones saw neither raider nor its attackers, but as he cycled along Middlesbrough's Marton Road and past St Luke's Hospital "the roar of engines and bursts of machine-gun fire sounded very close and loud above the cloud. The sounds died away in the direction of Eston Hills."

As it approached the hills which form Tees-side's southern boundary, the Junkers was trailing smoke and was low enough to prompt Bradford soldier Bill Greenwood, who had been enjoying a country walk up to that moment, to throw himself instinctively to the ground: when it passed over him, Greenwood caught a glimpse of the ventral gunner, Hans Steigerwald. Perhaps against all expectations, the ailing aircraft lifted sufficiently to clear the northern slopes and the summit to the west of the Nab tower. For some moments it seemed that it might continue its climb to a safer altitude and as it clawed its way upwards the ventral gunner made a "desperate bid for life and succeeded in jumping clear".

Thirty-nine-year-old Amy Watson was looking out of her aunt's window in Normanby when she saw the plane "flying over the hills from the direction of Middlesbrough – but then it suddenly dropped". The withering fire had finally taken its toll: the right engine ceased to function and the raider's nose dipped. The Ju88 plummeted earthwards in a terrifying spiral dive which was made even more frightening to nearby onlookers by the whining screams that accompanied it. As hikers on the summit scurried for safety when they saw the Junkers apparently about to crash on them, the plane struck the soft moorland above the Cross Keys Inn and exploded with such force that it created a huge crater and scattered wreckage over a 400-yard radius.

At about the same time, perhaps a mile to the west, Hans Steigerwald broke through the cloud over the woodlands flanking Flatts Lane and dropped earthwards, the parachute on which he had pinned his hopes streaming above him like a long ribbon.

Eleven-year-old Gerard Coughlan and his 14-year-old cousin had been walking close to the Normanby Brickworks in Flatts Lane when they heard gun-fire and had seen the Junkers in its dive. Believing that "it was going to crash on our side of the hill," they had started running down the lane towards Normanby. It was as they were passing Cross Wood that their attention was arrested by the sound of something crashing through the branches of trees some twenty yards to their left. On turning, they saw the

41 (Spitfire) Squadron personnel inspect the wreckage of Ju.88 4U+GH. Eston Hills, March 1941. (Northern Echo)

silk of a parachute, apparently extending from the tops of the thirty-foot trees to the ground. Close by, a crumpled body lay doubled up in a shallow stream: Steigerwald's "desperate bid for life" had failed. Schlott, Meingold and Schmigale did not fare any better: they were obliterated with their aircraft.

As the news of the bomber's demise spread, "hordes of people began streaming up the Normanby road and on to the hills. Many were youngsters, anxious for souvenirs. Twelve-year-old G. W. Skinn lived on Church Lane, Eston, and was one of many boys at that time who had boxes of shrapnel and anti-aircraft shell nose-cones collected after air raids: the Junkers was an opportunity just too rich to ignore. "Immediately news of the crash reached us, all the local boys made for the hills to scour the scene for fragments." But the explosive impact had been fierce and War's reality bared itself to him when he experienced the "horror of seeing small pieces of human skin and flesh clinging to the grass and heather". Seemingly, however, there were many souvenir hunters who were not deterred.

Although expressly forbidden, such was the scale of "collecting" that allegations were made that it was causing trouble to RAF Intelligence personnel who were attempting to investigate and to evaluate *Luftwaffe* equipment. Thus during the following days police toured local schools to appeal for the return of school-boys' "prizes" and to point out the illegality of such practices. It is not known whether such efforts were totally successful!

As was the practice of the times, Hans Steigerwald's body was interred in the RAF's own plot in Thornaby cemetery. He was buried alongside the graves of four of his countrymen who had crashed near Glaisdale in bad weather some five months earlier. Before the war was over, they would be joined by a further twenty-two *Luftwaffe* aircrew who were destined to fall from the skies over Cleveland.

March 1987. Twisted fragments of metal still mark the spot where Ju. 88 4U+GH crashed on Eston Hills 46 years earlier. (Author)

Feldwebel Peter Stahl, a Ju.88 pilot of KG30, believed that he and his crew carried out a lone attack on Middlesbrough on the night of 26/27 April, 1941, after diverting from Hull, which was blanketed by cloud. He describes his feelings thus:

"In the end I just have to give up (over Hull) and fly northwards in the hope of finding better visibility. Over Middlesbrough we can finally orientate ourselves beyond question, and I make my bombing run on the town. The AA defences are only moderate so that we can drop our explosive load quite accurately. On the way out, Hein and Theo report the flaring up of a fire. During our return flight over the North Sea I contemplate the sense or otherwise of such attacks. While I can rely on Hans to make every effort to find an important military target for our bombs, I also know that our terrible ammunition may have been unloaded somewhere where it would have had no effect at all. Then again, what if it has hit a residential district or even a hospital? This war really is a gruesome business."

(Peter Stahl: The Diving Eagle, *Kimber, 1984*)

Existing records make no reference to an attack on the night in question — but the raid of 15/16 April, 1941, does share common aspects with Stahl's account.

13

'TWO FLIES ON A TABLECLOTH' (MORPETH AND HOLY ISLAND, 6/7 MAY, 1941)

(Written in collaboration with Chris Goss)

In May, 1941, F/O Robert 'Bingo' Day and his gunner P/O Frank Lanning were the crew of a Defiant night-fighter of 141 Squadron, Acklington. During the first week of that month they experienced a particularly successful evening of operations.

Unlike the Beaufighters and Mosquitos that were to follow, the early night-fighters had no airborne radar and thus the successful interception of night-time raiders was a chancy business, heavily dependent upon luck and keen eyesight. Day and Lanning had both in good measure on the night of 6/7 May, 1941, when they intercepted three raiders and shot down two of them.

That night, bombers of *Luftflotten* 2 and 3 carried out a number of attacks on northern Britain. Bombs fell over the Tees and Tyne but the main thrust was against Glasgow and Clydeside.

Among the aircraft detailed to attack the Clyde was Heinkel 111H-5 (A1+CK); Werk Nu.3550) of 2/KG53, based at Vitry-en-Artois and crewed by *Unteroffizier* Karl Rassloff (pilot); *Gefreiter* Emmerich Lernbass (observer); *Unteroffizier* Karl Simon (wireless operator); *Gefreiter* Walter Schmidt (engineer) and *Gefreiter* Heinz Quittenbaum (gunner). Shortly before midnight, A1+CK was approaching the north-east port of Blyth at 10,000ft.

Day and Lanning (Defiant N.1796) had lifted off from Acklington at 11.25pm with orders to patrol Blyth to Seaham. After one unsuccessful interception, they were ordered to orbit Ashington. As midnight approached, they were flying south at 11,000ft: it was then that they saw a small black dot silhouetted against the cloud 1,000ft below. Its direction was westerly and "it looked like a black fly crawling steadily across a whiter-than-white tablecloth".

Day made a diving turn to starboard and positioned his aircraft almost underneath the bomber. Then, as was his usual practice, he slid back his cockpit hood to ensure a clearer view as he formated the Defiant 100ft below the target while his gunner sighted the four Brownings on the underside of the raider.

Three short bursts were sufficient to disable the Heinkel's port engine and set fire to the wing root. The victim dived away sharply, narrowly missing

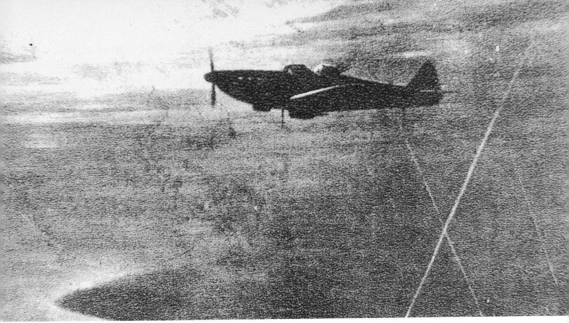

A Boulton-Paul Defiant night-fighter on patrol. (from the painting 'Stalking the night raider' by Roy Nockolds)

its attacker and spilling incandescent fragments as it spiralled earthwards. The Defiant followed, but *its* crew temporarily lost sight of the their quarry seconds later when Day was forced to take violent evasive action to avoid "running into what looked like a lot of frog-spawn suspended in space – the Newcastle balloon barrage".

Out of sight of the Defiant, and in spite of the fact that his aircraft was on fire and running on only one engine, Rassloff seemingly entertained ideas of reaching France: he turned his crippled craft round and headed seawards. At 11.57pm the RAF Wireless Intelligence Service intercepted Karl Simon's distress transmission: "CK returning. Engine damaged."

However, it soon became clear that a return to Vitry-en-Artois was out of the question. Minutes later Simon transmitted again: "Landing in England." After jettisoning his bombs, Rassloff settled his burning aircraft lower and eventually made a wheels-up landing in the grounds of St George's Mental Hospital, Morpeth, the five crew-members surviving without injury and apparently little the worse for their ordeal. Lanning and Day saw it crash in a flurry of sparks before they touched down at Acklington to refuel and re-arm.

The night was proving to be busy – "enemy aircraft kept coming in all over the place in singles" – and so at 1.15pm on 7 May, Day and Lanning were airborne once again. Some seventy-five minutes later they found themselves trailing a Ju.88.

Ju.88A-5 (4D+EN; Werk Nu.7177) of 5/KG30 was based at Gilze-Rijn (Holland) and was crewed by *Unteroffizier* Hans Schaber (pilot); *Gefreiter*

97

Heinz Nöske (observer); *Feldwebel* Paul Graupner (wireless operator) and *Gefreiter* Werner Arndt (gunner). They, too, had been briefed to attack Glasgow and their planned route would take them to the seaward of the UK's east coast as far as Berwick-on-Tweed then to the north-west of Glasgow before they dived towards the dockland target on a heading that would also start them on their homeward journey.

All had flown many operations over the UK but they had experienced problems only once — eighteen days earlier (on 19 April) when they had limped back to Gilze-Rijn on one engine. *Then* Fate had been kind and Schaber had managed to land safely, a feat for which he been awarded the Iron Cross 1st Class. Soon he would once again have to land his aircraft in difficult circumstances, but this time he would be a long way from home.

Precisely *where* the Defiant intercepted the Ju.88 is open to some doubt: the contemporary combat report submitted by Day and Lanning gave the location as five miles east of Seaham Harbour with the raider apparently on its homeward leg; Schaber claims that the interception took place within sight of the Clyde and the port of Glasgow *and before the bombs were dropped on the designated target.*

Such a wide discrepancy is hard to explain but there is little doubt that at 2.30am Lanning and Day were at 9,000ft when they spotted the Junkers "about half a mile ahead, at the same altitude and perfectly silhouetted against a bank of cloud, like a fly on a tablecloth".

The Ju.88 was flying at some 200mph and as the Defiant slowly overhauled its quarry, Day manoeuvred into position thirty yards below and parallel to the target's starboard side.

Lanning must have fired his first burst at almost the same time that Paul Graupner warned of Day's approach. He saw his explosive bullets strike home but observed no obvious damage to the target. However, the vibration of the Brownings was sufficient to throw Lanning's reflector sight out of its socket and against the interior of the turret, thus rendering it useless.

There was no reply from the German's guns as Schaber swung away left on the first of a series of gentle turns to port and to starboard, "the only evasive tactics by the enemy aircraft" to be noted by the Defiant crew during the engagement.

Day followed and positioned his aircraft almost as before so that Lanning could fire a second (unsighted) burst, again apparently without result. Thus Day resolved to get in close to allow his gunner an opportunity to fire at point-blank range.

As the Defiant drew nearer to the bomber, 'Bingo' once again threw back his perspex hood to ensure a clearer view and inadvertently jammed the muzzle of the lower right-hand gun behind the rear of the cockpit cover. By then the Junkers was very close but Lanning could not bring his guns to bear.

Pilot Officer Frank Lanning and Flying Officer 'Bingo' Day c.1941. (Frank Lanning)

By the time the difficulty had been overcome, Hans Schaber had half-rolled his aircraft, increased the angle of dive and then pulled back on the stick to end up flying in the opposite direction. Lanning and Day did not see the Junkers again. "Crestfallen and disappointed, we returned to base. Two bombers in one night would have been quite an achievement in those early days of 1941, and we (seemingly) had thrown away our chance. On the ground, we turned in our reports to the Intelligence Officer and then crept to bed – not to sleep, but to dwell on what might have been. We had, after all, missed an absolute sitter!"

But they were mistaken. One of Frank Lanning's bullets had made a critical mark; the Junkers *was* down.

Initially, everything seemed normal as 4D+EN made its escape, but then Werner Arndt reported that they appeared to be losing fuel and that the bomb-doors were stuck open. Hans Schaber immediately scanned his instruments and discovered that the temperature of the port engine was at its limits and still climbing: what the gunner had thought was fuel was, in fact, engine coolant. There was no option but to shut down the engine.

All four knew it would be virtually impossible to fly back to Holland on one engine and so attempts were made to lighten the load. All armament, apart from one gun and two ammunition drums, was jettisoned, as were the bomb-racks, which were blown off by explosive charge. Nöske even tried to remove the bomb-sight, but gave up after receiving repeated electric shocks. Then Hans Schaber trimmed the aircraft for single-engined flight and, following what they believed to be the southern shore of the Firth of Forth, headed towards the dubious safety of the North Sea.

The aircraft flew poorly, hindered as it was by the drag induced by the open bomb-doors. Gradually it lost height. By the time they reached Berwick-on-Tweed they were down to 200m and it was clear that they were not going to make it home. The thought of baling out into the darkness was unanimously rejected in favour of crash-landing on a beach. At the second attempt — the first being aborted on the sighting of an obstruction — 4D+EN slithered to a stop on the sand of Holy Island's north bay.

All were uninjured and Schaber ordered them into the darkness whilst he set the explosive charges to destroy his aircraft. It was to be the first of *four* separate (and unsuccessful) attempts to fire the bomber: the charge proved to be faulty; the firing of a flare pistol into the fuel tank failed to produce a flame; the use of the remaining machine-gun and ammunition did little more than produce holes in fuselage and wings; and the last resort — a petrol-soaked parachute set alight in the cockpit — burned for only a short time before it was extinguished by the wind!

Surprisingly, the crash-landing, the flares and the gun-fire failed to attract any attention from the island's inhabitants and the four had to wait until shortly after daybreak before a policeman and a civilian came over the dunes and escorted the four to captivity.

Postscript:

On 6 June, 1941, Frank Lanning and 'Bingo' Day were each awarded the DFC in recognition of their achievement. The nine German airmen survived the war and returned home some six years after their capture. Frank also survived and lives in happy retirement in the north of England. Sadly, 'Bingo' was killed on 18 June, 1944, while serving with 132 Squadron, Ford. He is buried in Connelles cemetery, France.

Night-fighter pilot *Oberfeldwebel* Wilhelm Beier of I/NJG2 who claimed to have shot down a Boulton-Paul Defiant near Thornaby-on-Tees on the night of 13 June 1941. Examination of local records produced no evidence of such an attack. (Simon Parry)

14

ENCOUNTERS WITH CLIFFS
(YORKSHIRE COAST, 9/10 JULY, 1941)

Arthur Coleman, retired sheep-farmer and ex-wartime auxiliary coastguard, will tell you that the cliffs behind his East Yorkshire village of Speeton can sometimes ensnare unwary sea-travellers, even those who might profess to know the area reasonably well. This is particularly so in the night hours, when the grey walls blend more readily with the blackness and allow the unsuspecting to get very close before realizing the danger. A trawler skipper who had once made such an unintended approach at night and who had suddenly found the cliffs looming ahead confided in Arthur that "we thought that the Devil had got us". But they were lucky: they managed to take evasive action in time.

However, Fate has not always been so forgiving: one night fifty years ago, sea travellers of a different kind had a less fortunate encounter at Speeton.

On the night of 9/10 July, a flight of three German Ju.88 bombers of *Küstenfliegergruppe* 106 took off from their base at Schiphol [Holland] with the intention of carrying out anti-shipping operations between Whitby and Holy Island. Each aircraft had a crew of four.

The lead aircraft [M2+AL] was being flown by *Hauptmann* Heinrich Moog; M2+CL by *Leutnant* Helmut Sinz and M2+EK by *Oberleutnant* Edgar Peisart. During the flight the raiders encountered mist patches off the English coast. Peisart, anxious to maintain his bearings, dropped to near sea-level and became separated from his companions.

As the three aircraft progressed northwards Peisart kept to seaward and would eventually reach his patrol line, but Moog and Sinz were unknowingly drifting west.

As they passed Flamborough Head they must have been very close to the coast, if not actually over it. They must also have been down to 100 feet of altitude for moments later the vague silhouette of a rocky wall suddenly loomed out of the mist and Moog found himself flying straight at Speeton Cliffs at some 280kph.

What happened next is not totally clear, but he did just manage to scrape over the top before his aircraft bellied into the fields immediately beyond. Alan Staveley, then a 15-year-old farmworker, had heard the Junkers' approach and is convinced that its engines were still driving as the aircraft gouged its way across one and a half fields before slewing through 360° and grinding to a halt.

Junkers Ju. 88s of the type that struck east coast cliffs on the night of 9/10 July, 1941. (Author's collection)

Sinz must have been to port of Moog's aircraft for he and his crew came to earth a mile or so further west. For reasons currently unknown, M2+CL was on fire as it settled towards the ground over Speeton village. Local legend has it that the planes had collided, but there is currently no evidence to support this belief.

At 11.48pm Arthur Coleman was in Wide Street, *en route* to report for his six-hour shift which was due to start at the coastguard station at midnight. He had stopped to chat with a soldier of the locally-billeted Royal Berkshire Regiment. They were standing outside the village shop, just below the track that leads to Jackson's Millholme Farm and the coastguard station beyond, when something attracted their attention.

> *"All I could see was the glow of a big ball of fire coming towards us through the fog. It was so low that we thought that it was going to land on us so we both dived to the ground. It only just passed over my head.... It put the wind up me, I can tell you.... And then there was a terrific crash from the direction of Philip Jackson's farm."*

Philip Jackson was due to go on shift with Arthur that night, but as the blazing Junkers was aiming for his house, he was still in bed: his sister was downstairs. Both they and their parents were to be exceptionally lucky that evening for Death missed them literally by feet.

The stricken plane took off the top of their barn and then careered across the front of their home, the starboard wing clipping one corner in the process. In virtually the same instant, the Junkers struck the ground and disintegrated in the field alongside the farmhouse. There were no survivors.

Philip's sister had seen the burning wreck fly past within feet of her window, but its true nature had escaped her. Believing the village was experiencing an incendiary attack, she shouted to her brother to get up without delay. Only when he got outside did Philip begin to grasp the significance of what had happened.

Among the smouldering debris that littered the landscape outside his house, he found a 'big bomb' just inside the field and four smaller ones that had been scattered on impact (he was to find out later that they had not been primed to explode). At the corner of the house lay the body of a crew member amid pieces of a charred parachute — a salutary reminder of War's waste.

Contrary to what might have been expected, he did not stay long at the scene: he was expected on duty at midnight and he knew that appropriate action was already being put into effect. He made his way to the coastguard station, where he was soon joined by Arthur Coleman.

In the fields above the cliff, Moog and his crew had survived their ordeal and were busily engaged in releasing their rubber boat. Having done so, and after their captain had set fire to his aircraft, they made their way to the cliffs with their dinghy, though no one seems quite clear as to their intention. In any case, they did not get far: Arthur had seen the diffused glow of the burning aircraft and had alerted the Army, but the Berkshires were already searching and the would-be escapers were soon apprehended.

The captured fliers spent some time under guard at the Speeton home of a Mrs Hartley, "a kind old soul who probably would have made them a cup of tea". Whether they got the tea is a matter of conjecture, but before they were removed early next morning the Germans made her a present of a silk scarf.

As they were driven away from Speeton, Moog and his crew might well have had thoughts for the friends they had lost — and for Peisart, who had sought to keep his bearings and had thus become separated, and safe.

What they could not possibly have known at the time was that Peisart and his crew had been dead for some hours.

It would seem that Peisart had reached the northern end of his patrol line and was on the south-bound leg when disaster struck.

Sixty-three-year-old Bernard Ward has lived in Cowbar, just across the stream from the North Yorkshire village of Staithes, all his life. He recalls that raiders destined for inland targets often crossed in over the small fishing village.

"On a still night you could hear them coming from Germany. Way out to sea. Droning for ages. Used to come straight over here. That night the air raid siren had sounded and I was outside the house. It was foggy.

I could hear the plane coming from the north; it was low and close inshore.

The sound of the engines, partly masked by Cowbar Nab as the plane approached, became much louder as he flew past the bay — then it was masked again. Then there was a crash and everything went quiet. A few seconds later, the smell of aviation fuel drifted back to us."

Whether visibility allowed Peisart to be fully aware of his position can only be guessed, but immediately after passing Staithes he banked to starboard, presumably once more to start his run to the north. His turn took him into Brackenberry Wyke, a small bay fringed by high cliffs just to the south of the village.

He may well have realized the danger and tried to climb out of it: a few feet higher and he would have succeeded. However, the tail unit clipped the cliff edge at the north end of the bay. The Junkers broke in two: the tail plummeted down the cliff; the rest disintegrated across the high shoulder of upland of Quarry Bank and the fields beyond. There were no survivors.

EYE-WITNESS

"As soon as I could get out of the house I went to the hilltop, where I joined some of my school-friends who were gazing up at Quarry Bank. We could clearly see the wreckage and much military activity. Some of us decided to brave the wrath of the teachers and go and have a look. On arrival at the site we could see that the aircraft was scattered across the middle of the field and was badly wrecked. The bombs it had been carrying were all against the bottom hedge and had rolled there on impact... The military guard from the Staithes Holiday Camp had erected a rope barrier round the wreckage and we were unable to get very close. It was said that the aircraft had hit the top of the cliff when flying in from the sea. On impact the aircraft must have simply disintegrated. Later I was able to see where it had struck. There was a deep indent in the edge of the cliff and it was filled with tiny pieces of perspex which we collected for souvenirs.

We were not punished for being late in school and after school we immediately rushed back to the site. We were kept well away from the aircraft by the guards who had to be on their toes because the area was in full view of the holiday camp and any observer using field glasses could see everything that went on. After several days, however, the guards became bored and less vigilant and we were able to sneak in and take parts for souvenirs. I collected quite a selection of small metal pieces but my prized exhibit was a small handle with a red knob which was labelled 'BEOBACHTER' which I now know to mean 'Observer'."

John Sherwood, school-boy, Staithes village, July, 1941

15

REDCAR'S DARKEST HOUR
(21 OCTOBER, 1941)

During the evening of 21 October, 1941, fifty German bombers operated over this country and attacked targets as far apart as Dover and Tyneside. Bombs were also dropped on Cleveland, some thirty high-explosives being widely scattered within the area described by Stokesley-Eston-Redcar-Loftus. Generally they fell in unpopulated areas and caused virtually no damage at all, but at 9.19pm two bombs exploded in a Redcar residential area, with dire consequences.

The siren had sounded at 9.14pm, but the eighteen members present in the Zetland Club, Coatham Road, had chosen to ignore it. As bombers were passing overhead – probably *en route* to other destinations, for there was little of strategic value in Redcar – the club was following a normal evening routine. Some members were gossiping at the bar; others were in a downstairs' front room where a bridge party was about to start a third rubber; upstairs a snooker game was drawing to a close.

Across the road from the club, local solicitor Harold Watson was more cautious: he, his daughter and their maid were in the shelter close by his house. A short distance away, the McIntyre family had taken refuge under a table in the cellar of their home in 46 Queen Street. Given the previous absence of raids on the town, they might well have felt reasonably secure – but then Fate took a hand.

As the *Evening Gazette* (31 October, 1941) was to put it: "The raid had been in progress for a little time and an anti-aircraft barrage was greeting enemy planes passing over the town. Suddenly one of the Nazi raiders swooped and unloaded a stick of bombs. Direct hits were scored on property."

Eye-witness Jim Cox was watching the raiders pass over as he stood in the garden of a house in Easson Road, less than a mile from the LNER station. He recalls that there was a train in the station and, as he looked in that direction, "there was a red glow in the sky – from the train's fire-box, I think – and this was followed by explosions in that vicinity." If Jim is correct, it would seem that the destruction that followed was directly attributable to a railwayman's carelessness.

ARP records show that two bombs were dropped (although contemporary newspaper reports refer to three): one struck the Zetland Club, demolishing it and surrounding properties; the second flattened 46 Queen Street.

One of the first on the scene was ARP Warden Ron Alexander:

"The siren had gone and I was on patrol in Queen Street with colleague Peter Escombe when we heard bombs screaming down close by. We both flung ourselves to the ground. There was a terrific bang, followed by a solid wall of dust that got in the eyes, the mouth and the nose.

When things settled down a bit we walked down Queen Street, seeking the scene of the explosion. We had to feel our way through the dust-filled air by using house bay-windows. Eventually, we came to the site where two houses had been flattened. There was a circle of destruction. In one of the houses, Mr and Mrs McIntyre and their six-month-old baby, together with an airman billeted with them, had taken refuge in the cellar. We found them all safe, crouching under a great mahogany table. All were transferred to the First Aid station — the old catholic school at the bottom of Queen Street.

Leaving Peter on site to complete the report, I made my way to the Wardens' Post (number 7) behind the council offices to notify them of the incident. I went from Queen Street into Elliot Street to Pierson Street, with the intention of going into Coatham Road. The Zetland Club stood on the corner of Pierson Street, just opposite the council offices. But when I got to the corner, I didn't know where I was: I couldn't see a thing and the roads were blocked with debris. I had to detour back-over to get back to Coatham Road and duly made my report.

It was then that I learned that two houses close to the council offices were down: Dr Robinson's (though no one was in it — Robinson was in the Zetland Club across the road), and the house of Mr Harold Watson, a local solicitor. He, his daughter and a maid were killed there.

I was instructed to help out at the Zetland, which had been severely damaged. Twelve people were killed there, a number of them being ARP officials who had been called to duty but who had stayed to finish their game of bridge. Mr Crozier (bank manager and a captain in the Home Guard) was called twice by 'phone to get with the Home Guard; Councillor Roebuck (shop-owner and commandant of special constables) was also called a couple of times, but he wanted to finish his game of snooker. Both were killed, as were Dr Robinson, Mr Ranson (a retired schoolmaster) and Alderman Harris, the mayor.

The Rescue and Demolition arrived and worked alongside the wardens (as did the Home Guard), clearing the site and attempting to rescue those in need. Eventually, we pulled them all out, one by one. Hartgrove's furniture vans were used as ambulances. The unlucky ones were taken to the mortuary at Redcar cemetery.

We worked through to noon the next day. We discovered Alderman Harris sitting in a basket chair below a large mirror. His eyes were wide open and he seemed to be all right, though perhaps shocked. I spoke to him but got no reply. As I got hold of him, he keeled over. He had been killed by the blast — but the mirror above him was untouched."

When the tally was finally taken, fifteen people had been killed, seven were sufficiently injured to require hospitalization and a further eight had suffered less serious injuries. It was a dreadful price to pay for a temporary lapse of the blackout.

"Here, I say, PRESS!"

The Battle of the Atlantic is being lost!

The reasons why:

1. German U-boats, German bombers and the German fleet sink and seriously damage between them every month a total of 700 000 to 1 million tons of British and allied shipping.

2. All attempts at finding a satisfactory means of defence against the German U-boats or the German bombers have failed disastrously.

3. Even President Roosevelt has openly stated that for every five ships sunk by Germany, Britain and America between them can only build two new ones. All attempts to launch a larger shipbuilding programme in America have failed.

4. Britain is no longer in a position to secure her avenues of supply. The population of Britain has to do with about half the ration that the population of Germany gets. Britain, herself, can only support 40 % of her population from her own resources in spite of the attempts made to increase the amount of land under cultivation. If the war is continued until 1942, 60 % of the population of Britain will starve!

All this means that starvation in Britain is not to be staved off. At the most it can be postponed, but whether starvation comes this year or at the beginning of next doesn't make a ha'porth of difference. Britain must starve because she is being cut off from her supplies.

Britain's losing the Battle of the Atlantic means
Britain's losing the war!

Not everything that was dropped by German raiders had physical destruction as its goal. This propaganda leaflet was part of a prolonged attempt to undermine the morale of the inhabitants of these islands: like similiar efforts by the British over Germany, the policy of persuasion had little or no effect. This particular example was dropped on Danby Moor (North Yorks) at 3.00 am, 18 July 1941. (A. Askew)

16

SPITFIRE NIGHTFIGHTER
(TEES-SIDE, 7 NOVEMBER, 1941)

Miroslav Antonin Liskutin was a Czech flier who served with 145 Squadron at Catterick from September to December, 1941. Early operational flights consisted mainly of convoy patrols, but in October '41 the possibility of the squadron being used to intercept enemy bombers on moonlit nights led to a series of individual 'fighter night' practices being introduced. Such night exercises consisted of two to three hours of night landings, with one or two flights towards the coast and back. The defensive patrol line was off the coast, east of Redcar, and north towards Hartlepool.

The following account from Liskutin's *Challenge in the Air* (Kimber, 1988) highlights some of the difficulties faced by night-time defenders in the days prior to the widespread use of radar-assisted airborne interception, initially in Beaufighters and later in Mosquitos.

MA Liskutin with Spitfire Vb. 312 (Czech) Squadron, RAF Harrowbeer, May, 1942.
(MA Liskutin)

"The night exercises were soon completed and a large-scale test was to be done during the next moonlight night. The intention was to launch twelve Spitfires into the night skies and they would take up a patrol line at 500 feet height separation outside Middlesbrough. The squadron was feverishly preparing for the try-out...but the call for our help came before we were ready.

One evening on a dark night [7 November, 1941], while off duty, I was with three other squadron pilots in the RAF Catterick Operations Room, just having a look at the situation and chatting up the charming WAAFs over a cup of tea.

Unexpectedly, there was a radar warning of some unidentified aircraft. This was quickly confirmed as enemy bombers heading for Middlesbrough. A few moments later Squadron Leader Turner, our squadron commander, appeared on the balcony above the main plotting room. Pointing to each of us individually he called: '10,000 feet, 11,000 feet, 12,000 feet, 13,000 feet. Vector 080. At your allocated level shoot at anything with two engines.'

Right from the start I could see that it was not a suitable night for any single-seater fighter operations, partly because of the complete darkness and particularly due to the weather. From the moment I set course I could see that the bombers were already dropping flares and the Middlesbrough area was alive with flashes of anti-aircraft fire. I still had some distance to go when the first bombs exploded in the harbour area. By the time I had reached my designated patrol position, the whole place below seemed to be illuminated with flares, fires and explosions....

Everything was set and ready as I took up my allocated post at 10,000 feet, keyed up and eager for my first encounter with the enemy, which seemed imminent.

The first thing to go wrong was the positioning. Apart from the fact that I was already too late and the bombers were over their target, I found myself, immediately after entering the designated airspace, in the immediate vicinity of intense anti-aircraft barrage. Obviously I was quite close to the enemy bombers but could not see anything. This nearness of exploding shells had a blinding effect on my night vision, which decreased my chances of seeing any potential targets. Very soon I realized that the allocated patrol line was much too close to Middlesbrough and would have to be changed for future operations, to make us more effective.

As I flew up and down the patrol line, the smoke on the ground and the cloud below me started obscuring the target area and I also started running into cloud at my allocated altitude. By then the other Spitfires above me would have been completely enclosed and, no doubt, have returned to base....In the rapidly deteriorating weather I could not possibly see the bombers. Also, losing sight of the ground, I might drift into the defended zone over Middlesbrough and could be shot down by our own defences! I felt very uneasy. Eventually, after some hesitation, I concluded that I had no option but to abandon my patrol and set course for base....

As I was setting course for Catterick I noted that the ground defences had stopped firing. This meant that the bombers were now out of their range. The night became pitch black again. Not a trace of light to be seen anywhere."

[M. A. Liskutin, DFC AFC: Challenge in the Air, *Kimber, 1988]*

Middlesbrough air raid records for 7 November, 1941, show that the attack commenced at 2210hrs and that some twenty high-explosives were scattered over a wide area of east Cleveland, where they caused only minor damage.

Sgt Pilot Miroslav Liskutin with Spitfire IIa (D-SO; P-8132) Catterick, September, 1941. (MA Liskutin)

A Luftwaffe Intelligence photograph of Middlesbrough, taken 4 September 1941. The picture clearly shows the Ironmasters' District, south of the Tees' loop, the ICI chemical plants, the North Tees power station, and the Furness shipbuilding yards at Haverton Hill. The 'craters' in the bottom left-hand corner are barrage balloon emplacements.
(Imperial War Museum)

17

'ANNIE' SNARES A GERMAN BOMBER
(CLEVELAND, 15 JANUARY, 1942)

Barrage balloons were an integral part of Britain's air defences during the Second World War and Tees-side had its fair share. Forty-eight of the hydrogen-filled gas bags – 62 feet long and 25 feet in diameter – were dotted in a random pattern over the area (including around ICI Billingham). The prime purpose of these 'flying elephants' was not to bring down raiders: their principal function was to keep enemy aircraft at altitudes which made accurate bombing difficult and to keep them at heights which allowed better targets for anti-aircraft defences and fighter aircraft. However, there were times when aircraft *did* fly into balloon cordons: sometimes they were lucky; sometimes they were not.

Any aircraft crew finding itself in such a predicament, particularly in darkness, was in a potentially very dangerous situation because collision with the cable which held the balloon in position would invariably stop the aircraft in its tracks and send it crashing to earth. Of course the Germans were aware of this and thus it was most unusual for any low-flying raiders to approach targets in darkness. Whenever bombers attacked Tees-side, which was usually at night, they generally flew at heights exceeding 5,000 feet. However, the occurrence on 15 January, 1942, was to prove a costly exception to the rule.

On that day Holland-based bombers of KG2 were detailed to launch a late-afternoon attack against shipping and port installations along England's eastern seabord. Among those taking part was a Dornier 217E-4 (Wk No.5314 U5+HS) of 8./KG2, crewed by *Feldwebel* Joachim Lehnis (pilot), *Leutnant* Rudolf Matern (bombardier), *Unteroffizier* Hans Maneke (radio-operator) and *Oberfeldwebel* Heinrich Richter (gunner).

Lehnis had been ordered to attack a convoy which was travelling 'eastwards off Middlesbrough' and thus it may well be that it was he who was responsible for the attack on the SS *Empire Bay*, which was bombed and seriously damaged further down the coast. But if that was the case then he also chose to seek inland targets. As dusk fell, a number of raiders crossed the north east coast. Lehnis was one of them – and he chose Cleveland.

At 5.30pm he dropped two high-explosive bombs on Skinningrove Ironworks, injuring eleven workers and inflicting sufficient damage to cause a serious loss of production. Twenty-five minutes later he dropped a bomb on Eston jetty, causing only slight damage to a railway line. Five minutes after that, his aircraft struck the cable of a barrage balloon flying 4,000 feet above the North Tees jetties — and within seconds the crushed remnants of the Dornier's tangled wreckage were blazing ferociously in a South Bank coal-yard: the charred remains of three of its crew lay nearby.

Some time after the event, the airman in charge of the site explained what had happened:

"It was just getting dark when we got orders to fly our balloon. In a few minutes she was off the bed and aloft. We were rather pleased with ourselves, the boys and me, for we had put it up in extra quick time. I remember saying to one of our blokes, 'If we don't get Annie up soon we'll probably be too late.' I was only joking, really, because we had put our Annie up scores of times before without even hearing an enemy plane.

Well, when she was up we trooped back to our hut, leaving the duty picquet on guard. We'd just started listening to the radio when we heard the plane coming low — very low, it was; much too low for my liking — so we decided to go outside and get a bit of cover. We'd no sooner got outside than the noise of the plane changed to a whine. It seemed as if it was diving right on top of us.

'Jenny Macke!' says one of our airmen — an Irishman who says things

The wreckage of the KG2 Dornier 217E-4 (U5+HS), which struck a Tees balloon cable on 15 January 1942. (Northern Echo)

like that when he's roused. 'Jenny Macke!' he says, 'he's going to machine-gun us.'

'He isn't,' says I. 'He's going to hit the cable.'

And he did. He went smack into it. There was a crash and the winch jumped as she took the strain. The cable sawed through the wing like a grocer's wire goes through cheese. That fixed him. Off came the best part of the starboard wing and we knew we'd got him."

The nine-foot section of severed wing fell into an adjacent balloon site: the Dornier was destined to travel not much further.

Mr C. V. Evans, warden of Grangetown Boys' Club, had heard the plane travelling eastwards "very low and very fast". When it collided with the cable there was a yellow flash and the engine note immediately changed. His first thought was that South Bank was going to be dive-bombed, but he was mistaken. Clearly out of control, the Dornier came screaming low over the housetops and then plunged into the coal depot at Clay Lane, South Bank. It crashed with a thunderous roar and in a sheet of flame which momentarily turned night into day; then it began to burn like a Brock's Benefit, its supply of Very cartridges popping off and arching skywards in a macabre fireworks display.

Instinctively, Evans ran towards the blazing wreck, but the heat was so intense that he could not get near. In any case, his was a futile gesture: the fliers were already well beyond help.

Back at the North Tees site the balloon crew were in jubilant mood as they celebrated their success with a cup of tea before they began to prepare a replacement for *Annie*. It took them until the early hours of the morning to put up their new balloon, but when they finally did get to bed they went feeling rather pleased with themselves. As they slept, the charred corpses of Joachim Lehnis, Rudolf Matern and Heinrich Richter were removed from the site and would subsequently be interred in the RAF plot at Thornaby's Acklam Road cemetery. Hans Maneke was never found.

It might well be that there was more than one *Luftwaffe* loss over the Tees that night for the Hartlepool lifeboat crew spent three hours searching Tees Bay after a score of red and white distress signals had been seen by Observer Corps and coast-watchers. It was generally believed that the signals were discharged by downed aircrew, but if that were the case then men and machine must have sunk without trace. It was a wild night and there was a high sea running: the search yielded nothing.

The crew of *Empire Bay* had better luck. At 7.30pm, as the balloon crew set about their task of replacing their charge, the Tees pilot cutter *W. R. Lister* slipped her mooring to answer an urgent appeal for assistance from the crippled vessel, which had limped into Tees Bay. A contemporary report of the incident by Pilot W. H. Young, at the time the skipper of the cutter, described what happened:

> *"The vessel had been bombed and seriously damaged. The* Empire Bay *was sinking but we were unaware of this fact. To locate the ship without lights under such conditions was a trying affair. Moreover, the cutter performed every gyration short of capsizing.*
>
> *After thirty minutes' steaming, a flame was sighted far away to northward. The course was altered and shortly afterwards we came upon* Empire Bay *plunging to her anchor and awash from quarter to poop.*
>
> *The Hartlepool and Tees examination vessel was in the vicinity and she contacted us by loud hailer, informing us that she considered it unsafe to launch either of her boats but that she would be willing to give us plenty of light by means of her searchlights if we intended any rescue. This we readily took advantage of and closed the* Empire Bay *on her starboard quarter very cautiously.*
>
> *After one or two determined attempts to wreck herself among the upturned boats, rafts, fathoms of lifeboat falls, and empty davits swinging drunkenly outboard, the cutter was coaxed alongside the quickly settling vessel.*
>
> *We were now on the starboard side, which was swept continuously by heavy seas, lifting and falling, crashing and jarring. But one by one the men jumped and fell aboard the cutter. Soon, they were safely aboard and, making them as comfortable as limited accommodation permitted, we proceeded towards the Tees entrance.*
>
> *During the whole of the above operation I was ably assisted by Tees pilots C. Gray, G. Pounder and J. C. Swinburne and my crew, including the engineer and apprentices Franklin and Cook."*

The matter-of-fact nature of this report belies the drama of the situation — and the danger that men were willing to face in order to go to the aid of strangers in distress. It was not a new phenomenon: others had performed similar acts before and others would do so afterwards. As it happened, the *Empire Bay* incident proved to be one of the most notable rescue feats effected by Tees pilots: it appears to have passed virtually unnoticed.

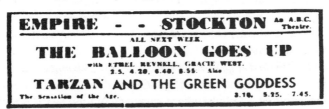

"The Balloon Goes Up *(Ethel Revnell and Gracie West). The antics of these two popular comediennes when they join the WAAF as balloon operators."*
This advertisement appeared on the Evening Gazette's *Entertainments' page, Saturday, 15 January, 1942. A strange coincidence!*

18

BEAUFIGHTER CREW
(SCORTON, 1943-1944)

Jeff 'Dinty' Moore was a Beaufighter pilot with 604 Squadron during their stay at Scorton (a satellite of Catterick) from April, 1943, to April, 1944. His NR (navigator-radar) was Jimmy Hogg. They flew Beaufighter Mk VI aircraft fitted with Mk VIII AI radar. The squadron's two Flights alternated their flying duties: two nights on/two nights off. 'Dinty' Moore's account of how Beaufighter crews trained to perfect their skills of interception provides an appropriate preface to S/Ldr Lewis Brandon's tale of an encounter with a Dornier 217 (See Episode 19).

"The crews would report to dispersal on the morning when their stint began, receiving their instructions and possibly doing night recognition training or tests. After lunch they would take up their aircraft for a night-flying test of about thirty minutes. If any snags showed up on the air test the ground crews would have time to service the faults — and a pretty good job they made of their tasks, I have to say.

After tea, depending on what time the sun went down, the crews would return to dispersal ready for the night's activities. Our job was to patrol the east coast from north of Whitby down to Hull. We operated in pairs (of aircraft) for up to three hours under the control of GCI (Ground Control Interceptor) stations. Seaton, Patrington and Goldsborough were the three GCI stations which controlled our patrols.

In the absence of an air raid we would practise interceptions on each other during the period of our patrol. The ground operators would try to bring the intercepting Beau on to the target Beau with a crossing flight at a range of approximately 7-8 miles. The idea of the crossing flight was to reduce the distance between aircraft more quickly and avoid a long stern chase with aircraft of similar speeds.

When our NR had a good clear contact on his airborne radar he would take over the interception with the word 'Contact' and would guide his pilot into the target using a fairly standard commentary used by all NRs.

From a range of 6-8 miles the target would be brought in as close as 300-400 feet, when the pilot would identify it visually — even on the darkest night. (Our night identification was of a high standard due to the fact that we trained regularly in a darkened room and, being competitive, we liked to get a high standard on tests.)

The moment the target pilot heard the interceptor aircraft declare 'Contact' that was the signal to start taking evasive action. Then a night-time dog-fight would ensue with the target trying to lose the interceptor. In this way we all became proficient at our job of night interception. A pairing with 'Wingco' Maxwell (the Commanding Officer and a 'fine pilot') on patrol resulted in a very hectic flight and one would often arrive back at dispersal after the flight with sweat running down one's back."

Bristol Beaufighter (Author's collection)

19

BEAUFIGHTER VICTORY (NORTHUMBERLAND COAST, 15 FEBRUARY, 1942)

Dornier 217s of KG2 were detailed to raid Sunderland on the night of 15 February, 1942. One of the aircraft taking part was a *Stab III* Do.217E-4 (U5+BD) crewed by *Leutnant* K. Pellar, *Major* K. Klostermann, *Feldwebel* H. Göggerle and *Unteroffizier* J. Uhl.

In February, 1942, peace-time film-actor Lewis Brandon was serving as an airborne-radar (AI) operator in a Beaufighter of 141 Squadron stationed at Acklington, Northumberland. At 7.50pm on the evening of the 15th, Pilot Officer Brandon and his pilot Flying Officer J. G. Benson claimed their first victory when they encountered U5+BD off the coast of Blyth.

Brandon's account of the incident is given in his highly readable memoir, *Night Flyer* (Kimber, 1961). He takes up the story shortly after his first (unsuccessful) attempted interception that evening.

'The Controller brought us back almost over Acklington, then the excitement started all over again.

"Hello, Rounder three-six. Blackbird Control. We have a Bogey for you to investigate. Turn port on zero one zero. Range five miles."

The term Bogey meant that we had to identify with extra care as it might be a friendly aircraft. Bandit meant that it was almost certainly an enemy. In either case positive identification was essential.

"Hello, three-six. Range now four miles, crossing you port to starboard. Any joy yet?"

"No, nothing yet," I informed Ben.

A second or two later it was a different story. A quite firm blip showed on both tubes, over to port and slightly below.

"Contact!" I called over the intercom. "Gently to port and go down. Range three and a half miles."

As Ben responded at once to my instructions he informed the Controller we had contact.

"Do you require any further help?" asked the Controller.

"Ease the turn now. Range three miles. No, I don't need any more help," I told Ben.

He passed that information on to the Controller and we went on to intercom.

Lewis Brandon as a Flight Lieutenant, 1942. (L. Brandon)

I could see that the aircraft we were chasing was still slightly over to port but the blip was slowly moving across the time base to starboard. We were flying straight now, so he was crossing us from port to starboard as the Controller had said. I could anticipate this and cut him off by turning now.

"Gently to starboard. Range two and a half miles," I told Ben.

"Gently starboard. I'm still going down."

"Level out now...Keep going starboard."

Thank the Lord he had reminded me of the height; I had been watching the azimuth tube too closely and had forgotten to watch the elevation tube.

As we levelled out, Ben automatically opened the throttles slightly to keep our speed constant. We were closing in perfectly. The blip showed almost dead ahead now.

"Steady now...Range one and a half...We're coming in nicely. Where do you want him?"

"Steady. Put him starboard and above. About ten degrees starboard. What range now?"

"Just under a mile. Throttle back slightly. Can you see anything yet?"

"No, not yet. Keep giving me the range."

"About two thousand feet. Gently port now."

A moment's pause, then explosively: "Christ! There it is. It's a bloody great Dornier. Here, have a look. I can hold it now."

I needed no urging but swivelled my seat around and peered into the blackness. My eyes took a moment to become accustomed to the dark, then I saw, just above and to starboard of us, the vague silhouette of an aircraft with pinpoints of reddish lights showing from the exhausts. I could see the pencil-thin fuselage and the twin fins. It was a Dornier 217 all right. Ben, who by this time was formating immediately beneath the Dornier and was only two or three hundred feet below, decided that the time for action had arrived.

The Dornier was weaving gently from side to side as it flew along. Ben throttled back very slightly and lifted the nose of the Beau. It was a little over to port now. It seemed strange that it should be completely indifferent to the presence of a Beaufighter so close. As it drifted in front of us, my heart was thumping so loudly it seemed impossible for the Huns not to hear it. As it passed through his gunsight, Ben turned the Beau almost imperceptibly to follow the Dornier. All hell broke loose as he pressed the gun button and four cannons and six machine guns banged and chattered away. The Beau filled with the acrid smoke and smell of cordite.

Ben had given it a two-second burst of gunfire; but although the Dornier began to lose height, we had seen no strikes. We did not use tracer bullets at night in order to retain the element of surprise. We were now following it down in a very sharp dive and Ben gave it two more bursts short bursts from about three hundred feet range. This time we saw strikes all along the fuselage and tail unit, from which there was a great red flash which illuminated the whole aircraft.

Ben was having a devil of a job to keep behind it now. We kept getting into the slipstream which threw us about violently. Before Ben could get another burst in, the Dornier had entered the clouds, diving into them at a very steep angle. We were about a thousand feet behind it by then and at a height of only two thousand feet Ben pulled out of the dive. We circled the spot where we had last seen the Dornier, hoping that we might see an explosion as it hit the deck. No such luck....

Later, in the crew-room, we were just taking off our flying clothing when the ops telephone rang. It was the Sector Controller to congratulate us and to tell the glad news that the Royal Observer Corps and Saint Mary's Lighthouse had independently reported a plane crashing into the sea four miles east of Blyth...The time and place coincided with our combat. We were told we could claim the Dornier as destroyed."

[Sq. Ldr. Lewis Brandon, DSO,DFC and Bar
Night Flyer *Kimber 1961,*]

The crew of U5+BD were never found.

20

A GERMAN AIRMAN REMEMBERS
(TEES-SIDE, 7/8 JULY, 1942)

On the night of 7/8 July, 1942, Dornier 217 bombers of KG2 were detailed to attack industrial targets on Tees-side. Among those taking part was *Oberleutnant* Werner Borner, a wireless operator with 4/KG2, who wrote the following account shortly after returning to his unit's base at Eindhoven (Holland).

Borner's narrative is of interest, partly because of his attempted explanation of the success of British night-fighters in intercepting raiders, but also because of his attitudes towards what some *Luftwaffe* crews came to call "the pilots' terror": the Z Rocket Projector.

The Z gun, also known as the UP weapon (unrotated projectile) had been introduced for high-altitude defence. It fired fin-stabilized 3-inch rockets which were 6ft 4inches in length, weighed 56lbs (including a warhead of 22lbs) and were fused to explode at a pre-set time after launch. Each rocket battery contained 64 3-inch twin projectors which launched a salvo of 128 rockets simultaneously. The missiles accelerated to 1,000mph in 1½ seconds before coasting to their maximum altitude of 19,000ft.

The device used the "scatter-gun" technique and was highly inaccurate. It was, however, psychologically impressive to both friend and foe alike. When the battery engaged raiders, 128 shells rocketed into the sky with a terrific rushing noise ("like an express train") before exploding in one thunderous, reverberating roar which rocked the area below; a lethal giant firework which bracketed a large expanse of sky with the brilliant red of detonating shells and unseen shards of potentially withering shrapnel.

The Tees defenders used the Z gun for the first time early in July, 1942. It was never successful as a destroyer of aircraft, but if Borner's account demonstrates the typical reaction of *Luftwaffe* crews to it, then the device might well have been more effective than was originally thought.

"Today we were sent yet again on the long trip which is also one of the most unpleasant, ie. to Middlesbrough. We don't like this region around Newcastle and Sunderland all that much. Firstly, there's the long hop over the sea, which is not good if the engine is ailing. Secondly, it is damned light up there in the perpetual phenomenon of the Polar or Northern Lights. The enemy fighters, on the other hand, like it very much. Thirdly, the English in

The Z gun…
…and its 'scatter-gun' effects. (Author's collection)

this area have a bright fireworks' spectacular during each air raid and no crew has yet ascertained whether it is a bluff or whether the sky really is on fire and full of iron when you fly through it. We only know that the "mortar man" as I, Oberleutnant Borner, have christened it, rises 700m into the air as a small fireball and then breaks up into hundreds of small bright shining projectiles which spread over a 45 degree sector, rise to 3,000m and there fizzle out. If you get in among that lot then you are beyond help — it's sharp ammunition you're talking about.

We have established that the "reloading" of this "ghostly cannon" takes about five minutes. So on reaching the coast in banked formation we wait for the next shot and then go in. In this way we have just enough time to avoid the trickery.

The most unpleasant thing about these long flights into enemy territory are the attacks by night-fighters over the sea. We soon found out that the English have stationed ships along the return paths of the night-fighters which act as guiding lights. We don't have another explanation. We have already seen too many German bombers explode before our eyes and break up and go down burning.

With this knowledge we took off on the night of 7 July at 23.42 hrs with a 4 ABB 500 [4 bomb cradles of 500 incendiaries]. We were to drop these on a munitions dump near Middlesbrough. The weather was as clear as a bell with excellent visibility.

At the Texel radio beacon we flew out over the North Sea. With mixed feelings we flew in a north-westerly direction towards our target. Four pairs of eyes scanned the skies for night-fighters: low-flying over water threatened danger from here on. At about the halfway point the famous trickery began. There were flashing signals from the sea which were repeated further in front of us. Apart from the droning of the engines and my continual warnings to watch out for night-fighters we were in a state of strained quiet.

Who would catch it today? "Master" Moese flies practice safety manoeuvres, not always straight ahead for that would have bad consequences. There! A long way in front of us was the sight so often seen along this coast: an aircraft exploding and burning pieces of wreckage floating soundlessly (for us) and ghost-like from a clear starry sky and into the water. Hopefully, a night-fighter shot down. Who would like to know?

Nothing happened for a while, then suddenly before us a short blast of fire with a visible tracer projectile, a dazzling glare of fire and a burning aeroplane goes down into the depths, apparently like a comet which glows in the earth's atmosphere. Only everything happens more slowly than with a shooting star of a comet. Our agitation is immense.

Are we the next? The whole war is a game of chance in every respect, and many a person today owes his life to this chance. Occasionally, we see more tracer bullets in front of us, but no more planes shot down. Then, on the northern horizon we see the ghostly glow of the Northern Lights. As well, the "Tommies" are getting at our comrades who took off earlier, with their fearful "mortar men". Immediately, I start the stop watch. Yes, they still take five minutes to reload. Now the brightness of the Northern Lights gradually becomes very unpleasant. In front of us we can clearly see the outline of a returning Do. 217. We can't be seen against the darkness of the south, bad luck if a night-fighter gets us from behind. Anxious moments of uncertainty till we reach the coast.

"Five more minutes to the target," I tell my Emil, whose face looks deathly white in the Northern Lights. He soundlessly nods "Understood". Course 270 degrees, so on course for attack. The release button is already lit up on my firing control panel. As the "mortar man" hasn't shown up, we fly round in fear but there's nothing going on. So let's get on with it: when all's said and done, we want to get back home.

Just before the target, it happens. A fireball comes towards us, bursts — and countless projectiles come towards us as if through a funnel. There's no chance of escape, we are right in the middle of this trickery, but we fly on and nothing happens.

Is it a bluff or not? We still don't know, nothing's happened to us. I press the release button of the bomb cradle and the incendiary bombs fall down, first of all turning over and over and then taking an oblique course towards the target.

The bombs seem to have found their mark as there are further fires. On the return flight, from 100km from the target zone we can see the glow of fires from two big explosions in the target area. Unfortunately, two planes do not return from this action."

The two crews that did not return from that operation were those of *Oberleutnant* Gunther Lanz (9/KG2; U5+BT) and *Feldwebel* Johann Grandl (4/KG2; U5+BM). Both Dorniers crashed in flames into the sea off the Tees estuary. They did not succumb to the 'pilots' terror' however, but to the guns of 406 (Beaufighter) Squadron, based at Scorton.

21

MIDDLESBROUGH'S HEAVIEST AIR RAID (NIGHT OF 25/26 JULY, 1942)

In the early hours of Sunday, 26 July, 1942, the wail of sirens, the dropping of flares, and the roar of gunfire provided the overture to what was to be Middlesbrough's most destructive air raid. Twenty-two Dornier 217 bombers of KG2 attacked in relays and dropped high-explosives, oil bombs and hundreds of incendiaries, seemingly with the intention of setting the town ablaze. It was on this night that the Co-op Victoria Hall, Linthorpe Road, was burned to the ground and the Leeds Hotel, Zetland Road, was destroyed by a direct hit. In terms of *physical* destruction of property, it was the heaviest and sharpest attack that the town experienced during the Second World War, and it lasted for just half an hour.

The scale of the destruction made it one of the nation's principal night attacks of 1942, and it was heralded by the dropping of red flares over Dent's Wharf, close to the Transporter Bridge, at 0.57am. The red flares that settled over the river band were followed three minutes later by white ones, first over Billingham then over Dorman's Britannia Works. The triangle so described embraced ICI and the town's Ironmasters' District, north of the railway station. Thus it would seem that the intended targets were industrial, but, as on previous occasions, it was to be the area south of the railway that would take the brunt.

The principal zones to be affected were the Wilson Street—Station Street area and the neighbourhood which embraces Clifton Street—Waterloo Road. Both zones suffered extensive damage due to high-explosives and fire-bombs but, in addition, incendiaries fell on other parts of the town, causing a large amount of damage to domestic and commercial properties and stretching the Fire Service, in particular, to its limits.

The dropping of fire-bombs was intended to destroy property, but their burning also acted as target markers for subsequent relays of attackers. Thus the risk presented by such weapons was doubly real and, consequently, ARP workers, firewatchers and members of the public were constantly alert to those which constituted potential risk. As one air raid warden was later to put it: "It looked as though people were waiting to catch them." However, not all were caught before they could inflict maximum damage.

Twelve minutes after the flares appeared over Dent's Wharf, the first

Middlesbrough Cooperative Stores, Victoria Hall, which stood at the junction of Clifton Street and Linthorpe Road prior to 25/26 July 1942. (Author's collection)

incendiaries began 'showering down' in the Newport Road area, near the Scala Cinema. While firewatchers scrambled to extinguish the burning phosphorus before property was endangered, the affected area was extended as more fire-bombs fell over the area described by Banks Street—Alexandra Street—Jamieson Street—Snowdon Road—St Paul's Church—North Riding Infirmary.

With the sounding of the 'Alert' the Infirmary staff had taken all movable patients to shelter. However, not all staff could go: some had to stay with the patients who could not be moved, while others knew that they would be needed to attend to the casualties that must surely arrive. Matron Miss Margaret Price and those nursing staff who stayed with her were later to be praised for the "splendid example they set to all by their calm bearing while bombs were falling," but they set an example in other ways too — for when fire-bombs began to fall all available hands played their part.

Some fifty such weapons fell in the grounds, usually to be put out by hospital maids who left the comparative safety of their shelters to extinguish incendiaries wherever they were seen to fall. Ten such bombs fell on the

Infirmary itself, threatening both the building and its occupants, until brought under control by staff, including Dr P. Baxter.

Baxter was House Surgeon at the Infirmary. When the attack got underway he left his bedroom clad only in pyjamas and dressing-gown and learned that three fire-bombs had dropped on the hospital roof. He scaled the drainpipe to reach them and found that fire was already taking hold. Using the girdle from his dressing-gown, and aided by helpers below, he hauled buckets of water to the roof and eventually got the outbreak under control. Having accomplished that, he sprained his ankle badly while making his way down to ground level. However, by that time raid casualties had started to arrive in some numbers and so he attempted to ignore his own pain while helping to treat those he felt had far greater need.

While Baxter was on the roof, the same spirit of selflessness was being shown 100 yards from the Infirmary, where women of the Middlesbrough Settlement, together with helpers, were to fight fires for three hours. The Warden, Miss Prinn, was subsequently fulsome in her praise of the twenty or so neighbours who risked the safety of their own property while the raid was in progress by rushing to extinguish fire-bombs. A nursery and some outbuildings were irreparably damaged but Miss Prinn readily acknowledged that without such instant help losses would have been much greater.

Incendiaries caused the first reported damage — at an ice factory in Brentnall Street, close to the Infirmary — but these were followed almost immediately by the first of 22.4 tons of explosives that were to fall on the area that night. Some fell noisily, with a whoosh or a whine that gave ample warning; others fell as quietly as snowflakes, supported by a canopy of silk that made no sound. One such parachute mine landed at the corner of Wilton Street and Waterloo Road eight minutes after the 'Alert' had sounded: its explosive force demolished six properties and caused some of the first casualties, a number of whom were trapped under rubble. Over the thirty minutes that followed, free-falling explosives shattered lives and property in Granville Road, Wilton Street and Albert Terrace.

Sailor Richard McGuigan, having experienced the terrors of dive-bombers in the Mediterranean, was taking a short leave at his home in Granville Road. When the sirens wailed he shepherded his wife and three children to the comparative safety of a public shelter and was returning home to get them warm clothing when a bomb screamed down to explode at the corner of Granville Road and Wilton Street. He was partly conscious when a would-be helper reached him: life left him as he gasped that even in the Mediterranean he had "seen nothing like this".

Arthur Grosvenor, in his off-licence in Granville Road, escaped serious injury by diving behind his counter as one high-explosive fell close to his premises. Though the blast flung a lethal combination of splintered glass and

Bomb-damaged shops in Wilson Street, some days after the attack of 25/26 July 1942.
The boarded up building on the left is the Wellington Hotel, which still occupies the site.
(E.Baxter/Evening Gazette)

broken masonry all around him he sustained only a slight cut to an arm. Seventeen-year-old Basil King, a warden on street patrol, was not so fortunate: he was killed instantly. Sadly, he was not the only one: Hector Pinkham, Michael Malloy and George Harris also succumbed.

A short distance away, at the Park Side Maternity Hospital, mothers and babies who were able to leave wards had been moved to safety – but one mother had given birth to a baby girl just minutes before the first bomb fell. With War's madness screaming all around, and bombs falling only yards away in Waterloo Road, the Matron and some of her staff kept vigil over their charges and went about their tasks as unperturbed as it was possible to be in such circumstances.

Gavin Kay and his family did not leave their home in Albert Terrace when the siren sounded. The bomb that exploded outside collapsed two-thirds of the building on top of them. Such was their luck that they all survived: sons Hugh and Walter were sufficiently injured to be detained in hospital, but their parents seemed to be little worse for their experience. As if to underline this, Kay, who was conductor of a number of local choirs, went on to conduct the Cleveland Harmonic Male Voice Choir at South Bank within hours of emerging from the rubble.

Another who was trapped in the debris of her home that night was 67-year-old Elizabeth Allen of 1, Waterloo Road. However, her predicament was more serious than that of the Kays. It took rescuers a long time to reach her and such was her pain that she was in need of medical attention long before she was able to be removed from the rubble. When an urgent request for instant medical aid reached the Infirmary at 2.45am it was Baxter who sought, and was given, permission to go.

Because of the pain he was suffering, he was taken to Waterloo Road on a stretcher. Upon his arrival he had to crawl down a hole cleared by the Rescue Squad in order to find the head and shoulders of Miss Allen so that he might administer an injection of morphia. His task completed, Baxter began to hobble back to the Infirmary. The pain from his ankle was excruciating, but the problem was partly eased when a policeman stopped him *en route* and, after questioning, loaned him a bicycle. On arrival at the Infirmary Baxter continued to treat raid victims.

Miss Allen was finally removed from the rubble at 6.00am and was admitted to the Infirmary: she died from her injuries six days later.

The Wilson Street area was the scene of the greatest devastation, with shops and offices suffering heavily. By 1.10am the area warden was reporting that Station Street, Hill Street, Crown Mews, Crown Street and Thompson Street had sustained 'very extensive damage' due to high-explosives; that water mains had been severely damaged; that fire had broken out and that access was very difficult due to blocked thoroughfares. The situation was destined to get worse.

One bomb struck close to the junction of Albert Road and Wilson Street, writing off some eight shop premises and striking the official quarters of five fire-watchers who had left only minutes earlier to open a number of offices for which they were responsible; another fell in Dundas Mews, trapping a number of persons and taking the life of Ernest Dunning; at twenty past one a 'heavy bomb' exploded behind the Grand Hotel, Zetland Road, and half the building collapsed into a mound of debris.

Vic and Margery Smith were caretakers of Lloyds Bank in Albert Road. They were sheltering in the bank's reinforced basement with their eight-year-old son, Victor, and though they knew that their protection was good, and certainly better than most, the violence, the noise and the vibration of explosions close by gave cause for fear and for doubt. They were to be among those whose luck would hold, but that was not to be so for everyone.

Trevor Wray's parents were the licensees of the Leeds Hotel at the junction of Linthorpe Road and Zetland Road. He was on leave from the Army and had delayed his return to camp on Saturday evening so that he could attend

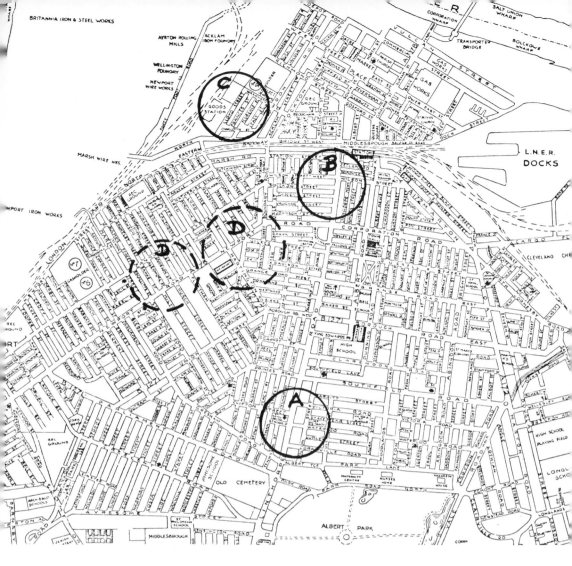

Air raid 25/26 July 1942: principal areas affected

Area A: Clifton Street-Linthorpe Road-Waterloo Road (mainly high explosive).

Area B: Wilson Street-Station Street (mainly high-explosive).

Area C: Goods station-Francis Street (high-explosive and incendiaries).

Area D: subjected to heavy concentrations of incendiaries. Neither C nor D suffered the level of material damage sustained by the other zones.

a dance at St Barnabas Hall: it was his intention to catch an early train on Sunday morning. When the siren sounded he had joined his parents and a maid, Mary Farrow, in the basement. At 1.32am the hotel was completely demolished by a direct hit which also tore away part of the already damaged Grand Hotel and completely wrecked Newbould's pork butcher's shop close by. The four were trapped in the basement: they were found to be dead when rescuers reached them four days later.

Shortly before the Leeds Hotel was hit, PC Bill Clare had occasion to seek Leading Warden Blakemore, who was not at his post at the junction of Station Street and Linthorpe Road. It was while Clare was at Blakemore's Linthorpe Mews house that the hotel was struck. Warden Blakemore was sheltering in one of the hotel's doorways: his body was subsequently found in the evening of 27 July under a slab of concrete which had collapsed on him.

The showers of incendiaries that fell in the North Road area were quickly followed by heavy calibre explosives. At 1.30am, Dorman, Long Britannia Works reported 'HE dropping all around,' but these were on waste ground, where craters were inconsequential. Others properties fared differently.

The oil works of Theo. Phillips suffered spectacular damage when a dozen oil storage tanks took direct hits and turned night into day. Luckily, there was no one in the works at the time and thus there were no casualties, but the blazing oil spilled into Lloyd Street and flowed down gutters to threaten those who had taken refuge in the street shelters. Occupants had to jump over burning oil in order to escape before being transferred to alternative protection on the Recreation Ground at Stockton Street.

Over the wall that separated Lloyd Street from the LNER Goods Yard, railway personnel were attempting to control a multitude of outbreaks that threatened to consume all. Incendiaries and high-explosives had fallen on and around the yard and 'fierce fires' had been started. In one or two cases, railwaymen living nearby ran to help deal with what was clearly developing into an ugly situation which could only get worse because flames were providing a target for enemy aircraft which could be heard overhead.

Arthur Bradshaw, of Pelham Street, was a shunter on shift that night whose efforts to minimize the effects of fire would earn him the British Empire Medal. As a later citation would say:

"With total disregard for his own safety he personally extinguished a number of incendiaries which had fallen into wagons and, although bombs were falling and there was heavy anti-aircraft fire, he worked with an engine to remove blazing wagons away from points of danger, thus minimizing the extent of destruction."

Much praise was subsequently bestowed on Bradshaw and on Yard Inspector Robert William Kitching for the way in which things were organized, wagons

A. Bradshaw.   R. W. Kitching.   Alb. E. Grace.   John Binks.

J. Charlesworth.   J. H. Jackson.   N. G. Reid.   J. McCluskey.

Eight of the LNER personnel of the Middlesbrough Goods Yard who received commendations for 'brave conduct' in Civil Defence during the night of 25/26 July 1942. (Evening Gazette)

unhitched and outbreaks prevented from spreading. In February 1943 Bradshaw was awarded the BEM and eight of his colleagues received commendations for brave conduct in Civil Defence.

At the time that 'very extensive damage' was occurring in the Station Street area, the southern end of Linthorpe Road was being subjected to a lethal combination of explosives and incendiaries, which caused extensive damage to domestic and shop property alike and caused at least three fatalities.

Florence Holmes, Norman Pringle and Frank Coley were voluntary fire-watchers at the Victoria Hall, which housed the head offices of the Middlesbrough Co-op Society and which stood at the corner of Clifton Street and Linthorpe Road. When the siren sounded they made their way to their stations and at 1.00am they were on duty at the top of the building and ready to extinguish any incendiary that might fall there.

Ten minutes later an oil bomb crashed through the roof and penetrated to ground level, where its 'burster charge' of TNT exploded on impact to ignite its main charge of highly-inflammable oil mixture. The three fire-watchers had little chance and were destined not to survive.

Councillor F. C. Pette, General Manager of the Middlesbrough Co-op Society and a Divisional Warden, was motoring to the Civil Defence HQ in

The Gables, Marton Road, when he learned that a number of shops in Linthorpe Road were ablaze. With some difficulty he made his way there, but on two occasions he had to leave his car and dive to the ground as bombs whistled down around him.

When he arrived at Victoria Hall the fire was taking hold on the ground floor. He went inside and attempted to salvage what documents and money he could before joining employees and others who were attempting to fight the outbreak, pending the arrival of the Fire Brigade. Such efforts, however, were to be of no avail: the flames spread greedily from floor to floor, from department to department, until the building was engulfed. Such was the ferocity of the outbreak that the blaze spread to adjacent premises and its flames swept across Linthorpe Road and set fire to Turner's paint shop opposite, together with properties alongside it. Then part of the Clifton Street wall collapsed on to the new Emporium that had opened only the previous year and that became involved, thus threatening some 200 people who had taken refuge in its especially strengthened basement. Fortunately, their evacuation was accomplished without loss.

The 'Clifton Street incident' developed into a problem of huge proportions which ultimately required forty pumps working for three hours to bring it under control. But such demands came at a time when the fire fighters were already severely stretched. Almost by the minute, urgent calls for help flooded into the Control Room:

"Fires at Dean Street and Adam Street. Brigade needed...Francis Street. Whole street on fire...Linthorpe Road occurrence. Large fire. Brigade wanted. Serious...Fire at 87 Duncombe Street out of control of fire-watchers...Fire, Gilkes Street and Buck Street. Urgent...Hurry Fire Brigade. Whole block burning at Ayresome Grange Road. Huge fire at ARP store, Snowdon Road. Urgent. Hurry."

And so it went on.

Exactly one hour after the first incendiaries fell, the Fire Service were attending incidents at sixteen separate locations. The situation had not eased by 3.15am, when the Brigade was attending forty pumps at Clifton Street; twenty pumps at Theo. Phillips, North Road; five pumps at Eaton's store, Newport Road; five pumps at Milton Street; fires at Station Street; Goods Yard; St. Paul's Church; Fleetham Street; Ayresome Grange Road; Grand Hotel; Millbank Street; Calthorpe Street; Wilson Street; Snowdon Road; Shaw's Foundry and Hartington Road.

Faced with such demands there were times when Brigade officials had to operate a scheme of priorities which necessitated re-directing appliances away from relatively less serious outbreaks to those which threatened more disastrous consequences. Even then there was no guarantee that help would arrive in time because the condition of roads blocked by debris did not favour speedy communications: in the case of Linthorpe Road, the stretch from Southfield Road to Borough Road was blocked by debris and from Southfield Road to Parliament Road by fire. Roads in other affected areas were hardly much different. Even when appliances arrived on site, damaged water mains meant that sometimes the means of extinguishing fires was lacking, while ruptured gas and electricity supplies brought the constant threat of additional hazards.

At least the Fire Brigade *knew* that their services were required and that their aim was visible. That was not always the case for Rescue Squads: they did not always have certainty on their side. For an hour after the first bomb fell requests for assistance were flowing into the Control Centre every five or six minutes. Some requests were based on fact, others on *suspicion* that persons were trapped under flattened buildings. In either case, crews had to be despatched to investigate, even though their services might not ultimately be needed. Although squads would be thankful when it was clear that their services were not needed at sites, such 'false alarms' did add an unwanted strain. By 1.55am the Rescue Department had only two squads left on stand-by and an appeal for reinforcements had to be made to Thornaby.

The pressure felt by the First Aid and Ambulance Service was perhaps even greater: for the first hour appeals for assistance were flooding into

The rear of the Leeds Hotel, at the junction of Linthorpe Road and Zetland Road, some days after the raid of 25/26 July 1942. (E.Baxter/Evening Gazette)

Control every two to three minutes. There was a danger of the Service being swamped and to offset that possibility appeals for reinforcements were made to Eston and to Thornaby less than an hour after the first bomb fell. Help was on its way within twenty minutes of the calls being received, but by then the pressure had eased markedly and in the event the additional teams were not used.

In fact, by 2.00am the worst was already over, though that may not have been obvious to those Civil Defence units which were heavily engaged in minimizing the raid's consequences. When condition 'White' was declared and the 'All Clear' sounded at 1.56am, the skies had been clear of enemy aircraft for some twenty minutes. The bomb that demolished the Leeds Hotel must have been one of the last to fall.

German sources claim that twenty-two aircraft took part in the attack and that they dropped 22.4 tons of high-explosives and 5.6 tons of incendiary bombs, from heights of 700 metres and 1500 metres. The raiders came over at staggered intervals, rather than in formation, but there is no guarantee that all of those that set out from Holland that night actually bombed the Tees area. However, those that did get through wrought sufficient destruction to engage the Civil Defence units for hours – in some cases, days – after the throb of aero-engines had faded.

With the coming of daybreak the clearing of debris from sites and streets was quickly underway, the Borough Engineer's squads being helped by locally billeted soldiers while members of the Home Guard assisted police in controlling traffic and the crowds of sightseers whose curiosity got the better of them. Some clearance works took longer than others: it was not until 27 July that Albert Road was open to traffic and not until 30 July that the last fatalities were located and removed – from the Leeds Hotel. While the crews at that place worked towards their sad discoveries, Bomb Reconnaissance officers were undertaking potentially very dangerous work as they investigated sites of suspected unexploded bombs in Newport Road, Crown Street, Britannia Works, Granville Road and Zetland Road.

Elsewhere, the families in shattered communities went about the task of trying to salvage household possessions from among the rubble and giving, where possible, a helping hand to those less fortunate than themselves. In two Rest Centres, Hugh Bell School and Ayresome Street School, which had been opened hours earlier to receive the homeless and those in more temporary need, accommodation was provided for some 530 persons who would need to be housed and fed until 28 July, by which time alternative arrangements would have been made.

On the evening of Sunday, 26 July, the following report was broadcast by the German News Service in Berlin:

What remained of Victoria Hall after it had been razed to the ground by an oil bomb. The building on the left is the Co-op Emporium, in the basement of which some 200 people were taking shelter. (E.Baxter/Evening Gazette)

"*German bombers raided the important British industrial town of Middlesbrough in several waves in the early hours of Sunday. Our bombers broke through the heavy barrage of anti-aircraft fire which protected the town in a circle.*

The strong barrage surrounding the town did not prevent our bombers from scoring numerous hits on the ironworks and harbour works. Heavy explosions broke out in the target area. They were followed by several large fires."

Given the positions of the flares, it seems highly likely that the 'ironworks and harbour works' were indeed the targets that night. However, the 'heavy explosions' did not always occur where they were intended: south of the Tees, only two industrial premises – Dorman, Long Britannia Works and Acklam Ironworks – suffered notifiable damage, and in both cases it was considered negligible.

Damage of another kind was far greater: sixteen people killed and fifty injured; sixty-eight houses and seventy-six business premises rendered uninhabitable and some 200 persons made homeless. In addition, some 1,000 houses and 220 business premises sustained minor damage.

EYE-WITNESS

"We were in the basement shelter of a shop in Newport Road, just opposite the North Riding Infirmary. Every now and again we could hear the distant crunch and thud of bombs and the pom-pom-pom of anti-aircraft guns. The noise was so bad that I thought that half the town had been blown up...I recall an elderly lady crying loudly. I was longing to have a look outside, but the cellar doors (wooden ones set in the pavement) were shut and there were grim-faced people standing nearby.

My father, who was a Corporal in the Home Guard, was outside for over an hour. When he came back he said that incendiaries had dropped on the Infirmary (some 50 yards from our shelter) but that they had been quickly dealt with. They had also fallen on St. Paul's Church and numerous streets... He never mentioned about the high-explosives that had been dropped in case of upsetting us, although I think that most of us heard them. Incidentally, it was sometimes difficult to distinguish guns from bombs."

A. W. Farrow, 16-year-old resident of Petch Street, Middlesbrough, 1942

EYE-WITNESS

"A stick of bombs and a land-mine wiped out a section of Wilton Street, where my grandparents lived. I was with my family in a shelter in Pearl Street and I felt the vibration when the mine exploded. Mr Fox, an ARP Warden in Pearl Street, knew that we had relatives in Wilton Street and so he told my parents what had happened. We all went up to see if my grandparents were all right. On the way, we saw that the Co-op and Turner's paint shop were on fire: it looked like Dante's inferno.

When we reached our destination we found that the land-mine had landed on the fish shop at the corner of Wilton Street and Waterloo Road and had taken out the whole block. I was very upset because I felt sure that my grandparents and their dog must be dead. When the siren had sounded the rest of the family had taken to the shelters, but grandad had stayed outside. He had seen the mine parachuting down and had dived into the house,

140

which was damaged by the blast and later had to be demolished. The whole family were safe — but grandad and the dog were much covered with soot."

A. Gillespie, 7-year-old resident of Pearl Street, Middlesbrough, 1942

EYE-WITNESS

"One night towards the end of July '42, both HE and incendiaries were used against Middlesbrough and the NFS were, in consequence, fully engaged. A heavy bomb had fallen just outside a large modern store, damaging the roadway and setting fire to the building. The huge fire which resulted demanded the attention of all available men and machines. Among the first on the scene was a column officer. Quickly he got out of his car to make urgent dispositions of fire-fighting appliances, and took two or three steps forward on to the wet, shining road stretching before him, its surface apparently unbroken. Suddenly he disappeared, and two firemen, looking down at the neatly filled crater at their feet, were rather amazed to see a steel helmet rise to the top of it, and still more surprised when they pulled out the helmet and found attached to it a column officer. There was no time to dwell upon the matter: he had been looking for water and he had found it; without pause he got two pumps to work from it."

R. W. Bell, Principal Officer, Regional National Fire Service, 1944

EYE-WITNESS

"July 25/26, 1942, was a bad night. There must have been over a hundred major fires. During the raid I went out with a Staff Officer who wanted to assess damage. We couldn't get up Linthorpe Road because there was a tunnel of fire from the Co-op stores to the shops opposite. It was near there that we found a woman who'd been blown double: her back had been broken and she had been folded in half. We covered her with a piece of cardboard. In the lower part of the town, where the flames from the Phillips' Oil Works fire were a hundred feet high, we came across a shelter that had a steel roof set on a low brick wall. A bomb had dropped nearby and its blast had lifted the roof and deposited it on the legs of the occupants. All were dead. During the raid I saw about four planes at various times. Being outside during a raid was dangerous. We found three lads wrapped round a lamp-post: they'd been out watching the bombing and had been caught by the blast. They were all dead.

We saw some strange sights too. Later that night I was with Mr Mardon (Chief Fire Officer, Middlesbrough) and we were on a roof in Wilson Street assessing damage. It was there that we saw a large tin of Heinz baked beans balanced upright on a chimney-pot, where it had landed after being blown three-hundred yards from Newbould's pie shop. We got a shock further down the street when we accidentally stood on a naked corpse. We didn't feel so bad when we realized that it was half a pig that had also 'flown' from Newbould's!"

Les Bennett, 30-year-old Leading Fireman, resident at Park Road South, Middlesbrough, 1942

EYE-WITNESS

"I remember walking up Linthorpe Road at the height of the raid with my friend, Ray Slater. We put out several incendiary bombs with sand-bags (which were positioned at street corners) on our way to the Co-op Emporium. On our arrival we saw that the flames were sweeping across the road and setting fire to the shops on the other side. When the Fire Brigade arrived we left. We learned later that one of our Air Training Corps Officers had been killed in the Co-op while fire-watching there (we were both in the ATC at the time and we both later joined the Air Force).

We walked back down Linthorpe Road, putting out incendiary bombs with sandbags as we went. We got a ticking-off from one motorist whose car bounced over one bag that we had placed in the road: I don't think he realized that there was a bomb under it... It seemed dangerous to run in to the road with a sandbag because after dropping the bag you were quite blinded by the brilliant magnesium flames and therefore it was impossible to see on-coming traffic.

We turned left into Princes Road and wended our way to Newport Road. Eaton's furniture shop was burning so we grabbed some buckets and gave a hand. Then an owner or manager of a tobacconist/sweet shop ran up and asked us to help him to put out his shop fire. We refused at first, because we were enjoying ourselves, but when he promised us free sweets and cigarettes we transferred our loyalties (and buckets) to his shop. After it was out, he did give us sweets and cigs.

By that time the AFS was at Eaton's with a trailer pump so we went down Farrer Street, under Denmark Street bridge and to the Lloyd Street/Charlotte Street area, where some houses were on fire. The AFS had been putting them out but then had been called away, perhaps to Eaton's or to the Co-op. They had left a line of hose and a nozzle connected to a hydrant, so we turned it on and put out the fires in the houses that we could reach with the jet. It was when I was unsuccessfully trying to dry my hands that I noticed that my handkerchief was covered with blood. I don't know how I had cut my wrist, but it needed treatment. I went along to the First Aid Post at the Holy Cross Church, Cannon Street, where the wound was duly stitched by a nervous girl first-aider who confessed that they were her first sutures (they subsequently turned septic). My name was duly entered on the casualty list, which caused a bit of consternation among my circle of friends because they all thought I'd been killed."

E. Reynolds, 17-year-old resident of Dale Street, Middlesbrough, 1942

July, 1942. Middlesbrough Corporation bus driver Ron Nelson and his conductor, Tommy James, pose for the camera while resting at Levick terminus before commencing their run to the "Transporter via Linthorpe Road". Within a month of this picture being taken, Ron Nelson was to have a narrow escape, at least from serious injury, when the blast from bombs dropped by a raider 'bounced his bus like a rubber ball'. (photo: Ron Nelson, M'bro)

22

LOW-LEVEL RAIDER
(MIDDLESBROUGH RAILWAY STATION,
3 AUGUST, 1942)

The way in

Bank Holiday Monday, 3 August, 1942, was a dull, grey day; there was a heavy cloud layer hanging low in the sky and there was a hint of drizzle in the air. Over the North Sea the cloud base was down to 200-300ft and the mass of grey was banked up to 12,000ft. Conditions were ideal for the hit-and-run tactics of 'pirate' raiders.

In the late morning some ten Dornier 217 bombers of II/KG40 took off from their Soesterberg (Holland) base and flew out over the North Sea. At 12.14pm they were picked up by Spurn Head radar. Nine subsequently crossed the coast between Spurn Head and Flamborough and flew inland to designated targets in the East and West Ridings of Yorkshire and the East Midlands: one continued to fly northwards.

At 12.24pm Pilot Officer R. H. Harrison, 406 (Beaufighter) Squadron, RCAF was scrambled from Scorton to intercept the north-bound bomber. Guided by Goldsborough (Kettleness) radar, Harrison made contact some 30 miles east of Flamborough Head, "where the enemy aircraft, flying at zero feet, jettisoned mines or bombs". After a short chase, Harrison managed to close to 500ft and straddle his quarry with gunfire before the Dornier broke hard to port and disappeared into cloud. Harrison lost contact, but when he requested assistance from Control he was ordered to follow a course almost immediately opposite to the one taken by the Dornier. He did not see it again.

For any aircraft flying northwards in the area mentioned, a change of course to port would lead towards land somewhere north of Scarborough. "At about midday," a Do.217 was seen four miles east of Staithes, tracking northwards and hugging the cloud base. Minutes later it crossed in just north of Saltburn. Sixteen-year-old Jim McNamara was spending a day on the Eston Hills with friends. They were sitting on the summit, close to the Nab tower, when they saw the aircraft cross the coast and follow the line of hills towards them. They watched, fascinated, as the Dornier circled over them a couple of times (so low that they could easily see the markings and the crew) before diving steeply towards the Warrenby Ironworks, a mile from

A Dornier 217 of the type that bombed Middlesbrough railway station (Author's collection)

the Tees estuary. They thought that the Works was the intended target, but then the raider banked to port and started to follow the river (and the railway line that paralleled it) towards Middlesbrough.

Roland Parkinson was an 18-year-old apprentice at Smith's Tees Dock. When the Works siren sounded, all the workers left the machine-shop where Parkinson was employed: the older men went straight to the shelters; the younger ones stayed outside.

> *"We were excited and there was a sense of adventure about it. The plane dipped out of the clouds above Smith's. It seemed to be heading for the river, then it banked, as if following the river. Its bomb-doors were open. Subsequently, we saw four 'dots' fall from the plane. A big cheer went up: we thought that he had been hit and the crew baling out. As the 'dots' continued to fall another cheer went up: we thought that their parachutes had failed to open. Then we heard the crumps and saw smoke. It was then that we realized that the 'dots' were bombs."*

Harry Hurst, sixteen years old, was a very young civilian aircraft-recognition instructor at the local RAF and RCAF stations. Some days before, he had received an updating of aircraft information from the Air Ministry, including details of the latest Dornier bomber, the Do.217E-2. On the morning of the attack he had been studying that information for the following week's training session at Thornaby aerodrome. He cannot remember now whether the sirens had sounded, but he had cause to leave his house in Westbourne Grove,

North Ormesby, to visit a friend in West Terrace, some 200 yards away.

"I hadn't gone far when I heard the unmistakable sound of BMW engines. The sound came from the South Bank area and the aircraft was obviously very low, travelling very fast and coming in my direction. My first sighting of it was when it broke cloud (the base of which was very uneven) almost directly over Cargo Fleet station. It was in a shallow dive and the bomb-doors were open. It made a long, sweeping turn to starboard, levelled out at about 600ft, and released its bombs when its was about over Schellenberg's hide factory. At its nearest I was within half a mile of it and I clearly identified it as a Dornier 217E-2, the first, I believe, to be seen in action over this country.

She was in the standard camouflage of day-bombers, ie. dappled bluish-grey on the upper surfaces and greyish-white underside. Immediately after releasing its bombs it banked slightly to port, flew level for a short time, then climbed back into the cover of the clouds. I heard the bombs explode although I could not see them, my ground vision being obscured by houses."

Ernie Reynolds was 17 years old at the time and an Air Training Corps cadet who was to complete twenty-nine bombing sorties over Germany as a Lancaster tail-gunner before reaching the age of 20. He was walking down Bridge Street East, towards the station, when he heard the drone of engines. When he saw the plane he immediately recognized it as a Dornier.

"It jinked and weaved as flak came up to it — I believe from a Royal Navy corvette in the docks. I stood open-mouthed and counted three bombs leaving the bomb-bay before I realized that I should be flat on the ground. I was lying on the pavement as the bombs whistled down."

P.C. Tim Felce was a 24-year-old policeman on the station 'patch'. As he walked up Bridge Street from Queen's Square his early morning shift was drawing to a close and his career with the police force was facing temporary suspension: he was due to join the Army the next day. He claims that the siren had sounded some time earlier, but when nothing had happened he had discounted it as a false alarm.

"It was a cold, misty kind of day and I was wearing my cape. I had just fastened my cape chain at the collar when I heard the sound of approaching engines. I thought that it was one of our returning bombers — we were on the flight path for Thornaby aerodrome. I was wrong. When it came into view, it was following a line from the river to the station. Its bomb-doors were open and it was extremely low — so low that I remember thinking that I could easily hit it with a cricket ball — and it was making a hell of a noise. Then I saw the bombs drop. Up the road from me was a civilian, standing and looking up at the plane. As the bombs fell I shouted to him to 'get down!' and then I flung myself to the ground, my fingers in my ears as a precaution against blast."

146

Ernie Reynolds in the uniform of the Air Training Corps, 1942.
(E. Reynolds)

Earlier that morning, Jim Cox, a Smith's Dock employee, had helped to tow a Royal Navy corvette from Smith's to Middlesbrough dock. Now his shift had ended and he was on his way home. After chatting to friends in Station Street he began walking towards the station, en-route for a bus that would take him home to Redcar. He passed the tailor's shop on the junction of Station Street and Linthorpe Road, but he could not have seen Peter Niman and William Thornelow who were working in there. However, he did notice "a lad working up a ladder," making repairs to the *Flying Angel* seamen's hostel on the opposite corner.

"When I was about fifty yards past the lad the noise of aircraft engines turned my eyes to the sky — we always looked up when we heard them. When I saw the plane it was racing straight towards me. I stopped and watched, wondering what were the four black 'dots' it was trailing behind it. When I realised what they were, I turned to run back up the street — towards Kirkup's warehouse."

The 'lad up the ladder' was Mr A. Franks, an employee of the local firm of Baker Brothers, who was repairing damage done to the hostel during an incendiary attack a week earlier. He had heard the plane's approach and had started down the ladder just as the bombs began to fall.

Mrs Pierre and her husband had intended taking their two young daughters to Redcar for a Bank Holiday treat that day, but because of the bad weather they had decided to take them to the cinema instead. Mrs Pierre suggested the Hippodrome, in Wilson Street (some 100 yards from the station); her husband preferred the Odeon. At 1.00pm she and the girls were in the Hippodrome, settling down to watch *How Green Was My Valley*. There was a certain irony in the title of the film showing at the Odeon: it was called *Reap The Wild Wind*.

As Mrs Pierre and her children settled down to watch the film, the 1.00pm train *from* Darlington was pulling into the North platform. Among the passengers who alighted was a party from Catterick village Women's Institute who were down for the day. One of their number, a Mrs Gregory, was spending her first day away from Catterick since the outbreak of war: until 3 August she had considered it too dangerous to travel. At 1.05pm that train continued its journey to Saltburn; at the same time the 1.05pm train *to* Darlington drew out from the South platform with a large number of passengers on board and many of the people who had been seeing off friends and relatives began to make their way towards the station exits; two minutes later a Guisborough train pulled out. The Saltburn train had travelled a mile and was nearing Cargo Fleet station when the raider flew over it.

The departure of the Darlington train signalled the end of Mark Motherdale's shift as ticket-collector. As the packed carriages disappeared

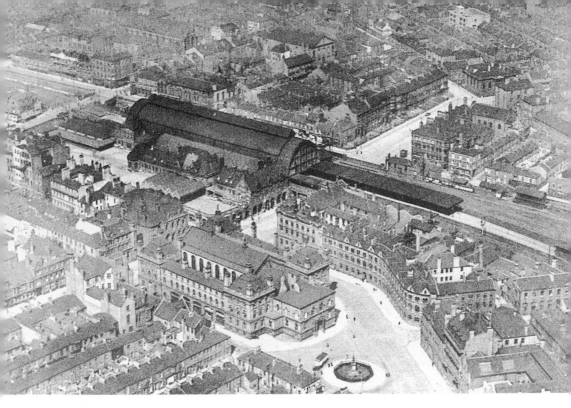

Middlesbrough railway station from the air, c.1925. (Author's collection)

down the line he walked to the collectors' office with the intention of leaving his tickets there before going home. He was expected home by 1.30pm at the latest — but at 1.08pm he was sitting in the office.

Seventeen-year-old Joyce Mason was working as an assistant at the bookstall on the south-side platform and was preparing to close for the afternoon. She decided to take some unsold newspapers back to the warehouse in Bridge Street: she left the stall minutes after 1.00pm. As she walked towards the subway which connects the North and South platforms, she may well have passed George Barrett, a merchant seaman on leave, and Timothy Carrol, both of whom were on the platform, waiting, perhaps, for the Newcastle train which was then pulling into the station.

Attendant John Bowes must have heard the train pull in as he mopped the floor of the gent's lavatory which was his responsibility. So also must Gladys Ripley and Hilary Squire, who were working behind the counter in the station buffet. With them was Charles Taylor, a 17½-year-old employed as a refreshment-room boy. While war always deals sad blows, it had been savagely

149

The west end of the station, from the Sussex Street crossing. The locomotive occupies the spot where the Newcastle engine stood on 3 August 1942. (Author's collection)

cruel to him: he had already lost five members of his family that year as a result of air raids.

Driver Tommy Marsden and his guard, James Binks, had brought the train down from Newcastle. After the passengers had alighted, Tommy had steamed into a passenger siding, uncoupled, and watched as another engine, driven by a Gateshead crew, pulled the coaches alongside the platform for the return trip north. The train was early: it was not due to leave until 1.20pm. Tommy stayed in the sidings, but James Binks chose to enter the station. He walked along the platform and to the engine, where driver William Buck and fireman D. Cowfield were on the footplate, chatting idly. Buck was on the platform side, directly opposite his 18-year-old helper. Binks may well have passed the time of day with them before he jumped down on to the line in front of the stationary locomotive and crossed over to the North platform.

He may even have seen Jim Davies, a Parcels Office worker, who was loading packages into the lift close by the engine prior to descending to the parcels subway which linked the platforms and which was located directly below the waiting locomotive. When the packages had been loaded, Jim stepped into the lift and reached out for the 'down' button.

Seconds before 1.08pm those people were preoccupied with the mundane tasks of day-to-day living, but things were soon to change. Ears pricked up to the dull throb of engines of a different sort, a throb which increased to a crescendo with frightening rapidity. When the raider screamed low over the station canopy the deafening roar of its engines gave momentary warning of what was to come. And although people in the vicinity may have shot apprehensive glances up towards the arched roof, there was no time to seek cover. The bombs were falling and the die had been cast.

The bombs fall

Four 500kg (1,100lbs each) high-explosive bombs were aimed at the station: they fell at 1.08pm. The first two scored direct hits. The third struck Kirkup's warehouse, demolishing it and the adjacent tailor's shop in which Peter Niman and William Thornelowe were working; they were both killed. The fourth destroyed five properties in Crown Street. The shock waves caught a Corporation bus, which had been halted by the traffic lights at the Zetland Road junction adjacent to the station, "bounced it like a rubber ball, shattered all of the windows" and threw conductress Ethel Clifford to the floor. Driver Ron Nelson heard no sound except the ringing of the bell, and then the nearby Albert Bridge "was moving and a curtain of rust was raining from it." The shock waves continued to radiate from the point of impact, shattering windows and ripping slates from the roofs of properties within a 400-yard radius. Reports came in that the Borough Road area had also been bombed, but that claim was subsequently disproved: it seems likely that damage there came from a different source.

The first bomb to hit the station ripped through the arched roof before exploding among the buildings lining the North platform: the blast, which was so powerful that it was heard in Darlington, tore a 15-yard gap across the entire width of the canopy. Extensive damage was caused to the refreshment-room, the ticket collectors' room, the guards' room and the general waiting-room − and flying masonry, shards of metal and slivers of glass joined with cascading girders and metalwork to form a lethal combination of hurtling debris which threatened anyone and anything exposed to it. The second bomb exploded immediately in front of the Newcastle train, the front buffer of which was later discovered 250 yards away in a house in Vaughan Street, and penetrated the parcels subway immediately below. The blast blew open the door of the lift which contained Jim Davies and flung him out. His clothing was shredded and he suffered extensive lacerations, but he refused to go to hospital on the grounds that there were others more in need of attention. Of the nine coaches which made up the train, three were completely wrecked.

As the dust was beginning to settle, PC Tim Felce was on his feet and racing to the ARP post in Lower East Street, from where he informed the Control Centre in Corporation Road before making his way to the site. He was to be involved in rescue work until 4.30pm. In times of crisis it is often

"The first bomb exploded among the buildings lining the North platform..." (Author's collection)

the trivial things that register. Perhaps when faced with scenes of devastation and horror, the mind focuses on the insignificant things in order to allow itself time to adjust. For Tim, the insignificances which remain locked in his mind are the memories of a locomotive brake-block "twisted like a piece of rock confectionery" and "a pair of false teeth lying among the debris".

Albert Farrow was struck by "the eerie silence" which descended upon the area in the immediate post-attack period, but other memories are also indelibly imprinted on his mind. As a 15-year-old, he had been on his way to the Hippodrome, but when the bombs fell he forgot about the cinema and walked round to the station. As he picked his way among the rubble he was confronted by the sight of a corpse lying below the platform; not far away, a pair of legs protruded from a pile of debris, around which a small band of rescuers were frantically working to release the trapped victim. Arthur did not stay.

Rescue work had begun almost immediately. Among the early helpers were a number of patrons of a nearby public house who were led by a steeplejack. In addition, workmen left their jobs and dashed to the spot and helped to release trapped victims. Within an hour that small group had been joined by 200 soldiers and the task of rescue got underway in earnest.

Driver William Buck, protected by the engine, was rescued alive and was allowed to leave hospital nine days later. Rescuers John Lister and Squad Leader Dodsworth had to tunnel for an hour and a half to free Mark Mothersdale from the rubble of the flattened collectors' office. His back was broken and he was destined to spend nine months in a plaster cast which reached from his neck to his hip. Gladys Ripley and Hilary Squires were extricated from the wrecked refreshment room without much difficulty and were allowed to go home after hospital treatment. Sadly, however, for some it was too late: fireman D. Cowfield, lavatory attendant John Bowe, George Barrett and Timothy Carrol all succumbed; young Charles Taylor became the *sixth* member of his family to die as a result of air raids that year. Guard James Binks should not have been at work at all; it should have been his day off, but he had changed shifts at the request of a colleague; his shift was due to finish at 2.00pm. He was killed in the station; the guard's van that he had left minutes before was unscathed.

Eight people lost their lives on that day in August and fifty-eight were

"...and tore a 15-yard gap across the entire width of the canopy..."
(Northern Echo)

Rescue-man John Lister who, with Squad Leader Dodsworth, rescued Mark Mothersdale from the ticket-collectors' office. (J. Lister)

injured, twenty-two of whom required hospital treatment. Of course it is idle speculation to consider what would have happened *if*...And yet the temptation to consider the part played by Chance can hardly be resisted. The movements of people within the station precinct seconds before the attack determined the final result; people's precise locations as the bombs were falling literally meant the difference between life and death. Some were lucky; some were not. Eight people died and fifty-six were injured, but the toll could have been far higher *if*...

If the raider had not been intercepted over the North Sea and *if* it had not circled over the Eston Hills, it would certainly have arrived over the railway station earlier than it did. Had it arrived three minutes earlier, there would have been three trains standing there and a large number of people on the platforms. In the event, those trains had left and most of the people who had been seeing off passengers had cleared the station before the bombs fell. Seemingly, Chance took eight lives, but it perhaps saved many more, including that of Jim Cox.

When the bombs exploded, the blast laid him flat and a relatively light debris of masonry and metal crashed down on him, shredding the oilskins he was wearing. When he eventually managed to stagger to his feet, the street was strewn with rubble and a dense cloud of white dust was working its way up the road. Across the way, an ATS girl, bleeding from the head and screaming hysterically, was being comforted by two men. Though sore and bruised, Jim was not seriously hurt and he subsequently managed to pick his way through the rubble and caught his bus home. He later learned that Kirkup's warehouse had received a direct hit. Ironically, the blast that laid him flat had probably saved his life. He was lucky, but since that day he has often found himself wondering about the fate of "the lad up the ladder".

Mr Franks had started down from his perch as the bombs were falling. He had not reached the bottom before the blast caught him and he was buried under rubble. The hostel was damaged and had to be evacuated. He has no recollection where he landed, but he did suffer multiple injuries and when rescuers finally reached him they used a door as an improvised stretcher and put him on a passing builder's wagon, which took him to the town's North Riding Infirmary.

Mrs Pierre and her two daughters did not experience "the excitement and sense of adventure" felt by more distant observers. When Crown Street was hit the explosions were less than one hundred yards from the Hippodrome.

"The noise was deafening and the whole place shook violently. Some of the people made a mad dash for the exits, which were blocked by usherettes who tried to calm them down. I didn't move: I was terrified — but I didn't show it because of the girls. Then the manager got up on the stage and told us that everything was all right."

When she and the girls eventually left the cinema, barricades had been erected

Taken shortly after the attack. The closeness of the second explosion to the engine is clearly apparent. The stretcher party is carrying the body of the guard, who was killed on the platform. (E. Baxter/Evening Gazette)

and rescue work was underway. Her husband, in the Odeon, never heard a thing.

Joyce Mason was particularly lucky. She was in the subway when the bombs struck. The kiosk she had left a very short while before was demolished by falling girders which had been blasted from the canopy by the bombs' explosive force.

The attack caused much structural damage to the station but not sufficient to disrupt its operation for any length of time. Priority traffic was immediately re-routed, freight traffic was restored within 25 hours and passenger services were back to normal some eight hours after that. Within fifteen minutes of the raid LNER, working with Middlesbrough Corporation Transport and the United Bus Company, had started to organize a shuttle service to local stations for would-be rail passengers; the Star and Garter Hotel, Marton Road, was the picking-up point. Among the first in the queue was Mrs Gregory. She returned to Catterick at the first available opportunity and she did not leave the village again until after the cessation of hostilities in 1945.

The way out
Ron Hartas was working on No. 3 Rolling Mills at Dorman, Long's Britannia Works, one mile west of the station.

"Around dinner-time the siren on the Mill office sounded and we made our way to the concrete shelter which was on the wharf side, exactly opposite the Billingham Reach Wharf. As there was no gunfire we just stood around outside the shelter. It was a very grey day; very low cloud. All the barrage balloons were up, although we could not see them. There were several of them around the steelworks on the south of the river and several more on the north side, around ICI. Suddenly we heard the explosions, and within seconds the German plane passed over our heads. It couldn't have been more than 200-300 feet high. There was a rattle of gunfire, but who was shooting I don't know. We ducked: we thought he was shooting at us.

The plane went straight across the river, over Billingham Reach Wharf and passed through the balloon cordon. He must have been very close to hitting one. Then he disappeared in the direction of Billingham."

Mr D. Conlin was living in Billingham and was standing in the garden of his parents' home in Conifer Crescent. He remembers that the Dornier:

"came low over Billingham Bottoms, skirted Norton church and curved over Billingham. The sirens had sounded. Then the local Ack-Ack let go. No wonder he kept low, the metal that was thrown up at him shook our end of Tees-side somewhat. He must have been looking for the sea because he made off in the direction of Cowpen Marshes."

Seconds later, Mr J. Berry saw it dip out of the clouds over Haverton Hill as

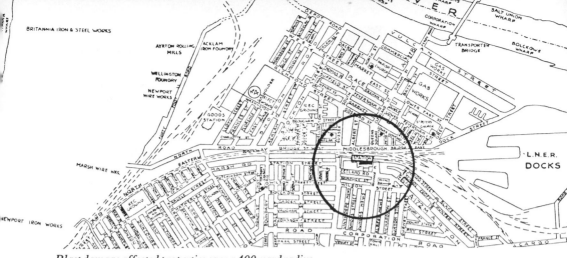

Blast damage affected properties over a 400-yard radius.

it flew in a south-easterly direction towards the coast. At about that time, Saltburn resident Mrs Campbell and her friend had finished taking coffee at the Saltburn Spa and were preparing to leave:

"As we came out of the door a large, low-flying plane came over the Spa from the land and flew out to sea. After that the 'All Clear' went and we realized that the warning must have gone while we were inside. Shortly after, we learned that Middlesbrough station had been bombed."

The raider was on his way home.

Defences caught napping?
If the raider had been hoping to achieve a measure of surprise, it would seem that he was more successful than might reasonably have been expected. In view of the fact that Tees-side was considered to be "quite heavily defended" *and* that he had been intercepted off Flamborough, it is a tribute to the pilot's skill and tenacity that he got through at all. Clearly, luck played its part and no doubt so did the weather conditions, but one cannot help thinking that confusion among defenders was also a contributory factor.

The re-directing of Harrison's Beaufighter *away* from the route taken by the Dornier, seemingly much to Harrison's surprise, is just one example; the failure of Fighter Command to alert other interceptors may well be another. There also appears to have been much confusion with regard to the sounding of warning sirens. Mrs Robinson, an ARP Warden in Redcar at the time, distinctly remembers having her washing day interrupted by *two* 'Alerts' and *two* 'All Clears' *before* the raid got underway, while in other parts of the area it seems that warnings sounded too early, too late or not at all, as is evidenced by eye-witness accounts. Similar confusion arose in respect of the response of anti-aircraft defences. Almost equal numbers of eye-witnesses spread throughout the Tees area claimed that the guns in *their* area *did* or *did not*

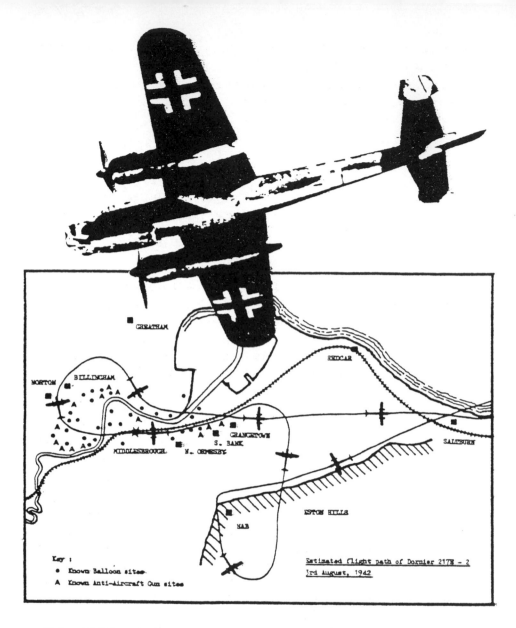

Estimated flight path of the D.217 that bombed Middlesbrough railway station,
3 August 1942.

open fire. The truth would seem to be that *some* gunners did respond, but, with the exception of the corvette in the docks, after the raider had passed.

George Matthews, a signalman at the Eston West signal box some six miles from the station, had been overflown by the Dornier on its way in, low enough for him to glimpse the missiles ready to drop from the open bomb-bay.

He is adamant that no shots were fired from the gunsite on the nearby Works' tip at South Bank:

> *"It transpired that the gunners were waiting for orders to fire. The commanding officer had gone to lunch and did not know about the raid. Subsequently, the situation of command was moved to the gun posts."*

Harry Hurst is equally certain that there was no gunfire before the bombs fell:

> *"The Dornier was back in the clouds before local batteries opened up. When they did, the shells were bursting low over North Ormesby [one mile south-east of the station]. As this was well away from the route of the Dornier, I thought that another aircraft was about and I was anxious to get a look at it. However, I neither saw nor heard another aircraft and can only assume that the shells had gone past the track of the Dornier, the fuses having been wrongly set, and hence exploded where they did."*

When Harry returned home he was surprised to find his living-room bay window smashed and smoke coming from the room. A cautious inspection revealed an unexploded rocket shell lying on the carpet!

Twenty-four properties in the town sustained damage as a result of 'friendly' shrapnel or unexploded rockets, but this was wholly to slate roofs and glazing and was of a minor nature. It seems likely that unexploded rockets falling in the vicinity of Borough Road prompted some observers to believe that that area was also under attack. The next day (Tuesday, 4 August, 1942) the Middlesbrough *Evening Gazette* reported that as soon as the guns opened up "the raider promptly disappeared". This attributes more to the role of the artillery than was actually the case. The German left because his task was done; there was no point in hanging around any longer.

Postscript

There is an intriguing postscript. Following publication of extracts of this account in the Middlesbrough *Evening Gazette* in August, 1986, I received a letter from a reader whose mother had visited the German town of Kassel in 1950. While there she went into a handbag shop to make a purchase, during the course of which she fell into conversation with the owner, who spoke fluent English. He asked her which town she was from. When she told him that she was from Middlesbrough he replied that he knew the town well, having bombed the railway station there in 1942, while searching for ICI. If that is the case, there is the puzzle of why he did not attack the chemical works, which he must have been able to see a mile or so beyond the station. Indeed, within seconds of bombing the station he flew *through* the balloon barrage which hung over the Billingham plant.

23

DUEL OVER NEW MARSKE
(CLEVELAND, 6 SEPTEMBER, 1942)

Although British Home Defence Forces could not have known that the Luftwaffe had designated Sunderland as a primary target for the night of 6 September, 1942, suspicions that the north-east had been targeted might well have been aroused earlier that day when two German reconnaissance aircraft visited the area in the late morning. The visitors were Messerschmitt 210s of *Erprobungstaffel Me.210* (16/KG6): 2H+HA flown by *Oberleutnant* Walter Maurer (pilot) and *Feldwebel* Rudolf Jansen; and 2H+CA crewed by *Feldwebel* Heinrich Mösges (pilot) and *Obergefreiter* Eduard Czerny.

The weather was almost perfect for photo-reconnaissance — slight haze at sea-level, a few scattered clouds at 5,000 feet but otherwise clear sky and excellent visibility — and the intruders might well have been grateful for that. However, perhaps such feelings of gratitude, if they existed at all, were tempered by the realization that such clear skies meant increased risk of interception should fighters be alerted.

In fact the 210s had been detected by radar while they were still well out over the North Sea and twenty minutes before they reached the English coast two Typhoon fighter interceptors were already on station and waiting for them.

New Zealander P/O Perrin and P/O Bridges of No.1 (Typhoon) Squadron had been scrambled from RAF Acklington at 11.16am. Under Ouston Control, they patrolled northwards to the Farne Islands before swinging south to Blyth. From there, off shore and on a bearing of 190 degrees, they paralleled the coast towards Tees-side.

It was 11.40am as Maurer and Mösges approached the north-east coastline. As they did so, Mösges edged his machine closer to that of his leader and both aircraft began weaving, presumably as a defensive manoeuvre against a surprise attack. But even as the intruders drew closer together, Perrin and Bridges established a visual contact. At 28,500 feet and to seaward of Redcar, the 210s were already being followed.

When Perrin and Bridges spotted their quarry the latter were flying north-west. As their pursuers turned hard to starboard and gave chase at a range of 1,500 yards the 210s turned west to cross the coast close to Redcar, where they escaped heavy anti-aircraft fire. When the Typhoons had closed to 1,000 yards the raiders were over Lackenby. It was then that Maurer must have realized the danger, for Perrin saw him jettison bombs before

Messerschmitt 210s (Author's collection)

both enemy aircraft broke steeply outwards. Perrin dived in pursuit of Mösges while Bridges broke hard right to follow Maurer.

Closing to 250 yards, Perrin managed a two-second cannon burst from astern and slightly to port, damaging the intruder's port engine in the process. He then crossed over to fire another two-second burst from astern and slightly to starboard. Pieces flew off the raider's engine as the shells found their target.

Mösges and Czerny must have known then that the game was up. If they had any doubts, these were dramatically dispelled moments later. Perrin rapidly began to overtake the now faltering 210, and when he fired his third

Hawker Typhoons (Author's collection)

and final burst it was from 100 yards, decreasing to 50 from dead astern. The effect was to blast away part of the tail unit and to cause flames to lick around what remained of the rudder. The stricken craft turned on its back to commence a vertical dive earthwards at full power.

Perrin followed, but soon he found that he was diving too fast. In turning to keep sight of his victim, which had now dived beyond the vertical, he 'blacked out' at 23,000 feet when his airspeed indicator was registering 520mph. At 3,000 feet the tail of the Messerschmitt broke off just forward of the leading edge of the fin and the plane started spinning to its final fate in the manner of a sycamore seed.

Eight-year-old Stanley Hill lived at New Buildings Farm, New Marske, and had spent part of the morning with his father in their garden, gathering vegetables for Sunday lunch. It was while they were strolling back to the house that they heard the muted stutter of cannon-fire directly overhead. Stan squinted skywards to see the two aircraft playing their deadly game high above, one seemingly tied to the tail of the other by an invisible thread which ensured that the writhings of the pursued would be mirrored by the pursuer. It was a game played largely in silence, for the machines were too high to be heard, but even to the eight-year-old the *thump-thump-thump* of cannon-fire could have only one meaning.

When the doomed raider went into its vertical dive it seemed that it might strike the farmhouse and so Stan followed his father's instructions to run into the middle of the field and away from danger. When he finally stopped running and once again turned his eyes to the sky it seemed as if *everything* was falling: the aircraft was still tumbling, and high above that the severed tail was fluttering towards the ground that it would take 'ages to reach'; but what really caught his eye was what seemed to be a falling 'dot'. As the 'dot' took shape, Stan realized that one of the crew — it must have been Eduard Czerny — was falling to earth "feet first and ramrod straight, as if standing to attention, and with his parachute Roman-candled above him".

Whether Czerny had baled out or whether he had been ejected by his aircraft's gyrations can only be a matter of conjecture. The same might also be said of Heinrich Mösges. It would appear that he had struggled to regain control of his machine because Stan remembers that the aircraft appeared to flatten out over New Buildings Farm and glide low over the small reservoir nearby as if preparing to land, albeit upside down. As it passed over the water "the second man came tripping out of the air and plunged into the middle of the pool a split-second before the aircraft tucked into the ground and stopped dead just beyond the north wall of the reservoir".

As the eight-year-old started to run towards the water, Eduard Czerny plummeted into the field, midway between the farmhouse and the pool and some 100 yards to Stan's left. It was the flier's twenty-third birthday — and his parachute had failed him. Whether Heinrich Mösges actually survived *his* fall is academic: there were eye-witnesses and would-be rescuers on site within a short time of the crash, but none could get on to the reservoir

September, 1942, the crumpled remains of Me.210 2H+CA lie in a field close to New Buildings Farm and the Redcar reservoir, New Marske. The tail unit eventually came down in the field seen between the trees in the upper right of the picture. (Author's collection)

premises because they were sealed off from public access. By the time they had gained access and retrieved Mösges from the water he was dead.

Perrin saw little of these events for he had 'blacked out' and his aircraft was screaming towards the sea off Hartlepool. When he came to, his altimeter was registering 3,000 feet and the water seemed to be approaching at an alarming rate. More worrying, perhaps, was the violent hammering noise emanating from somewhere on his aircraft. As he eased out of the dive he thought that the Typhoon must have been damaged and that he might well have to bale out. Thus he called Ouston Control to 'fix' his position. It was then that he noticed that one of the safety catches had come out of his starboard cockpit door, thus causing it to vibrate in the aircraft's slipstream. Relieved, he set course for Acklington. On route, he was joined by his Blue 2, Pilot Officer Bridges.

Bridges had pursued the second Me.210 as far as Robin Hood's Bay before finally putting paid to it. It crashed at Sledgate shortly after its crew had baled out. Jansen landed quite close to the village and was captured by Frank Roberts, a journalist on the *Hull Daily Mail*, who was holidaying in the area; Maurer landed in the sea, where he was picked up by the crew of the Scarborough motor coble *Florence* who landed him at that port hours later.

The New Marske wreck remained on site and under guard until the following Wednesday. By that time, of course, the bodies of the Germans had been removed. Like others before them, they were accorded full military honours when they were buried in the RAF plot in Thornaby cemetery, where they still lie.

Postscript:

The above account was included in an illustrated lecture I gave to members of the Cleveland Family History Society on 4 March, 1992. In the audience was Mary Atkin of Middlesbrough who, as a seven-year-old had witnessed the shooting down of the Me.210 over New Marske. Perhaps the following extract from the letter she subsequently wrote to me makes a fitting postscript.

"I remember that Sunday morning so well. It was a glorious day, more in keeping with simple countryside pleasures than the fight-to-the-death pursuits I witnessed. I can realize that now, but at the time, watching it with my parents and neighbours in Wardman Crescent, Redcar, it was an exciting victory. We, the 'goodies' had won the battle and there before our eyes the enemy came tumbling down to the ground. We cheered. Later that week I heard my mother saying, 'He was only a young boy.'

To the child I was then, that Sunday morning was more or less the extent of my war. When I heard your talk I suddenly recognized my bit of the war — and I felt remarkably ashamed of my behaviour. I was surprised to hear about Heinrich, a second victim of whom I had been ignorant, but as a mother now of a 23-year-old son I felt close to Eduard Czerny — the 'young boy' I had remembered for 50 years. I just had to go to the Thornaby Garden of Remembrance, to kneel by his grave and to pay my respects.

The day I visited, the skies were not the beautiful blue I associated with the day of the crash, but overcast to match my spirits. As I reached the secluded little corner of the cemetery, peaceful and well cared for, it started to rain. It was moving to recall the event 'face-to-face' so to speak. Perhaps to the gardener there who politely acknowledged my presence, the tears on my cheeks were only raindrops."

Czerny and Mösges were buried in Thornaby Cemetery. Czerny's forename has been wrongly stated and his friend's name has been anglicised. (Author)

24

DEATH OF A DORNIER 217
(Tees-side, 11/12 March, 1943)

On the night of 11/12 March, 1943, the *Luftwaffe* raid on the north-east had Newcastle as its primary target. However, as on other occasions, some aircraft made their landfall further south, and bombs intended for destinations to the north fell elsewhere.

Tees-side had two 'Alerts' that night: at 9.42pm (seemingly to no effect) and at 11.16pm, the latter being the preface to what was later officially described as "a light attack on the area," during which a small number of high-explosives were scattered over the district.

German Pathfinder units had been given the task of illuminating targets for following bombers, but it would seem that a number of markers were clearly off track. Ben Wise, then of Manor Farm, Little Stainton, remembers that:

"From Sunderland to Tees-side there was a mass of blue, yellow and orange lights — parachute flares. There seemed to be hundreds of them. It was a beautiful sight."

One minute before Middlesbrough's second 'Alert' sounded, a chandelier of eight flares was falling to the north of the town's Newport Bridge and was the signal for the start of a very severe anti-aircraft barrage. During the following six minutes white flares were dropped over the Newport gasometers and over Thornaby while to the south-west yellow was the chosen colour.

As luck would have it, no bombs fell on Middlesbrough that night but three casualties occurred in Linthorpe when an anti-aircraft shell landed in Westbourne Road, its explosion fatally injuring two firewatchers and seriously injuring a third. In addition, a young girl was slightly injured and superficial damage was caused to four houses. Anti-aircraft shells were also responsible for problems elsewhere in the area, including extensive damage to a barge moored in the Tees opposite the Graving Dock and the demolition of a bungalow in Saltburn.

At least three bombs fell on South Bank. One dropped harmlessly on vacant land alongside the railway line near Skipper's Lane; another exploded on vacant land close to the fire brigade sub-station and a row of houses at the bottom of Normanby Road (close to the railway station), causing some structural damage and a number of casualties due to flying glass; the third landed in a street alongside the police station, its destructive force disrupting power supplies and creating sufficient debris to block the Middlesbrough road for two days.

Providentially, there were few serious casualties, but two were to prove fatal. Police Superintendent W. H. Wilson and his family lived in the rear of the police station. When the third bomb fell in the street alongside, part of their living quarters was wrecked. Mrs Wilson and a daughter were severely injured by bomb fragments. They died the next day. Three other members of the family who were caught in the explosion suffered chiefly from shock.

In total, South Bank's casualties amounted to two killed and thirty-one injured, eighteen of whom required hospitalization. Ten properties sustained serious damage and a further 140 houses were rendered temporarily uninhabitable. One hundred and five of their occupants had to be given short-term accommodation at four Rest Centres, including Mission Hall, Grangetown, and Normanby Road Methodist Chapel.

Exactly how many explosives were dropped on Thornaby is a matter of conjecture. However, the resultant damage was enough to ensure that the attack was considered to be the heaviest experienced by the town.

Two parachute mines fell at 11.33pm. One landed at the corner of George Street and Thornaby Road. It demolished the Britannia Hotel and four adjacent houses. Just three minutes before, the six members of the Devine family, occupiers of the hotel, had left for the safety of the shelters. *They* survived, but others were not so lucky: Warden Miriam Pugh (40) was struck down in the vicinity of the hotel, while Robert Hornsby (75) died among the rubble of his home at 23 Thornaby Road. A third victim, John Lambert (65), succumbed in Princess Street when the second mine made a direct hit on the electricity sub-station there.

EYE-WITNESS

"Cloudless night. Searchlights grand. Guns awful. AA shell dropped in Westbourne Road. A good few enemy planes over. Thornaby got it badly at 11.30. Land-mines dropped."

Diary extract for 11 March, 1943. Jim Davidson, resident of Oxford Road, Middlesbrough, 1943

The destruction of the sub-station cut off power to a number of industrial plants in the vicinity, including Head Wrightson's. There it was expected that the stoppage would last at least twenty-four hours, would affect 4,000 employees and would cause "a serious loss of production". Other firms in the area, notably Chas. Kinnel & Co. and the Bon Lea Foundry, suffered temporary suspension of operations due to 'extensive damage', while Cleveland

Flour Mills, close by Victoria Bridge, had to curtail activities during the hours of darkness because of blast damage to their blackout precautions. (Given the distance of the Mills from the impact points of both mines, it may well be that this blast damage was attributable to additional explosives, accounts of which have since been lost.)

The following day the *North Eastern Gazette* was to report that:
"a spectacular feature of the raid over the North-East...was the frequency with which German planes were caught and held by concentrations of searchlights, the displays made by such being considered to be the most striking of the war in the north" to that time.

At least one such interception was made over Thornaby, where a large number of searchlights held a raider in a cone of light for some time. It was clearly seen by spectators, some of whom claimed that it was struck by AA fire before making out to sea.

It was during a heavy anti-aircraft barrage that curiosity got the better of Bill Stephenson, a Tynesider lodging in Lawrence Street, Stockton. When the barrage was at its height he went outside to see what was happening and was killed at the junction of Lawrence Street and Yarm Lane when a bomb fell within yards of him. The same explosion wrecked a watchman's hut nearby: its usual occupant, John Miller, of Nolan Street, Stockton, had vacated it only a short time before and was unscathed. A further two bombs fell near Wreford's Farm, Newham Grange, but their effect is unknown.

As mentioned earlier, Middlesbrough did not experience any bombing that night, though a number of flares did fall in the vicinity. The first dropped (possibly by an aircraft of II/KG2) to the north-west of the town at 11.15pm, one minute before the second 'Alert' and was the signal for the opening of a most severe anti-aircraft barrage.

For Tees-sider Albert Farrow, that first chandelier of light "turned night into day" and for one *Luftwaffe* Pathfinder crew it gave the first indication that they were being pursued by a night-fighter.

The Scorton-based Beaufighter of 219 Squadron was crewed by F/Lt John Willson (pilot) and F/O Douglas Bunch (navigator-radar). They had already been airborne for some three hours, none of which had been without incident.

Leaving Scorton at 8.40pm for Ground Control Interception (GCI) practice, they had soon been directed to intercept raiders off the coast. Following an inconclusive encounter with a raider near Newcastle at 9.30pm, they had destroyed one Do.217 four miles east of Cullercoats twenty-four minutes later and were very probably responsible for another that crashed into the sea off Hartlepool shortly before 11.00pm.

It was within minutes of the encounter off Hartlepool that Ground Control gave Willson another contact, a 'bogey' that might not be an enemy. Initially, the contact's low altitude (7,500ft) and slow speed (130mph) almost fooled the Beaufighter crew into thinking that it was a friendly bomber returning from operations. But then the contact increased speed to 220mph and commenced climbing. Willson eased in behind and followed: at 13,500ft he positively identified his 'bogey' as hostile.

EYE-WITNESS

'The whole area was lit up like daylight by German flares... and of course our searchlights were very active. I always remember my mother saying: "What a marvellous sight — if only it were for peaceful purposes".'

Alf Ward, 18-year-old farmworker, Little Stainton, 1942

Willson's quarry was a Do.217E-2 [UB+BL; Werk Nu. 4541] of III/KG2 crewed by *Oberleutnant* Ernst Schneiderbauer (pilot), *Unteroffizier* Johann Weber (radio-operator), *Unteroffizier* Martin Hoffmann (observer) and *Oberfeldwebel* Gregor Eilbrecht (mechanic): they were *en route* to Newcastle and had crossed in over the Tees only seconds earlier.

Schneiderbauer recalls that:

"I had the task to mark the target by parachute flare bombs and HE bombs. Time of the attack was 23.25hrs. After a low-level flight across the North Sea until a turning point 50km south of Newcastle, I climbed up to a height of 3300m, flying special figures as a defence against radar and night-fighters."

He continued his 'special figures' (later reported by Willson as "violent evasive action in a series of dives and climbs to port and starboard") as he progressed along the Tees towards Darlington. However, such manoeuvres did not prevent him being caught for a few seconds by a cone of searchlights over Stockton. Nor did they shake off the undetected Beaufighter.

Willson, at the minimum of range of 600ft, was within striking distance, but he refrained from attack because he would have to use deflection shooting: he held his fire, hoping that the Dornier would steady up. However, his hand was forced seconds later. The Dornier began to circle and because it was nearing the area where incendiary bombs were burning, Willson edged closer and prepared to shoot.

By then they were approaching Little Stainton, some five miles north-east of Darlington and some ten miles north-west of Middlesbrough. However, Schneiderbauer thought that he was elsewhere:

"We were above the north-west part of Newcastle. Here I opened the bomb-bay doors and began the gliding attack. Suddenly it was like daylight when Pathfinders of II/KG2 dropped their flare bombs and my radio-operator, Hans Weber, shouted 'Nightfighter coming in from the right!' I sharply turned down to the right."

Ernst Schneiderbauer poses in front of the aircraft that crashed at Great Stainton. (via Chris Goss)

Willson was then 400ft behind and, while turning to starboard in pursuit of his quarry, he 'pulled the sight through the E/A, giving a deflection shot of 2 seconds." His burst of fire damaged the Dornier's tail-plane and cut its way diagonally through the raider's canopy from right to left, destroying the left windscreen (its splinters causing a slight injury to Schneiderbauer's left eye), the dashboard, the EiV and the left engine, but miraculously, leaving the crew (apart from the pilot) unscathed.

With the left engine and the tailplane out of order, Schneiderbauer ordered his crew to bale out while "I stabilized my plane by using the rudder and the trim... trim compensation and the aileron." After some difficulty with the escape hatch, the four managed to evacuate seconds before their aircraft dipped towards the vertical.

Harry and Minnie Wall lived at 'Wayside' just across the road from the entrance to The Grange, in the County Durham village of Great Stainton. They had heard the wail of sirens and were lying alert in their bed, half-dressed and with everything ready, including their pet cats in a basket, for a speedy evacuation should that prove necessary. That moment came when they witnessed Willson's interception, "which seemed very close".

Military personnel examine what is believed to be the wreckage of the Great Stainton Dornier, March 1943. (Northern Echo)

They had no shelter of their own, but their parents had a dugout at their home alongside the Old Rectory and so the Walls resolved to go there. As they rushed downstairs the crippled raider must have been passing low overhead, spilling fire as it went. When the Walls reached the landing window they saw that the area between 'Wayside' and The Grange was ablaze, perhaps as a consequence of fuel spillage.

As the couple hesitated momentarily, the Dornier dived into the ground and obliterated itself in the field behind The Grange, its explosive impact gouging out a crater 16ft deep and 30ft in diameter, and creating an extremely fierce fire that fed greedily upon the parachute flares and explosive incendiaries that had been destined for the Tyne.

The four fliers landed within a half-mile of their burning aircraft. Schneiderbauer crashed through trees in the grounds of The Grange, contusing his knees and breaking his left shoulder; a short distance away, a colleague landed in the trees in the grounds of the Old Rectory and remained suspended there until he was eventually rescued by the local Home Guard; another landed some 400 yards from the village and was subsequently apprehended on the Stainton road by Darlington fireman John Wilson, who was *en route* to the burning wreckage. Hoffmann, one of the first to bale out and who broke a leg on landing in a field midway between the two Staintons, was not found until some time afterwards, when men of the Stillington Home Guard organized a systematic sweep of the area.

Postscript

The four were destined to spend the remainder of the war as POWs in Canada, from where they returned to Germany some two years after the cessation of hostilities. Schneiderbauer and Weber are still alive but Gregor Eilbrecht and Martin Hoffmann died in 1988. Of the Beaufighter crew, John Willson continued flying Beaufighters until August, 1943, when he was reported missing some 25 miles north of Algiers. Bunch survived the war and died in 1982.

The Dornier's escape hatch still survives at Little Stainton. (Author)

In April, 1943, 604 (Beaufighter) Squadron re-equipped with Mk VI aircraft and moved from Ford (Sussex) to Scorton, a satellite of Catterick. Their role would be the defence of Middlesbrough and Hull. Among those who made the journey northwards was Jeremy Howard-Williams and his NR (navigator-radar) Tony Nordberg. They would stay at Scorton for four months before being re-posted on completion of their tour of operations.

> *"We had anticipated a quiet time at Scorton, but we were mistaken. The Germans were raiding Hull and Middlesbrough often enough to keep us in a state of expectancy every night. We in B Flight, however, got to the point at which we knew that the* Luftwaffe *would not come over when we were on the programme; with unfailing regularity the enemy came when A Flight was at readiness.... From our arrival my log book contains an almost monotonous succession of entries for the next two months: NFT followed by CHL. That is to say we tested our aircraft during the day and then flew an uneventful night patrol on a low-looking Chain Home station."*

(Jeremy Howard-Williams: *Night Intruder*, David & Charles, 1976)

Following his arrival at Scorton, Howard-Williams had to wait two months before seeing his first German aircraft — while on a two-week exchange at Coltishall with John Quinton, a temporary replacement NR.

Jeremy Howard-Williams

On the evening of 12 June, 1943, they intercepted a low-flying Ju.88 off the East Anglian coast and pursued it eastwards for ten minutes. Fire was exchanged a number of times during the encounter, even though the range never fell below 1,200 yards. Howard-Williams broke off the engagement when his ammunition was exhausted. Although he was sure that hits had been scored, the Ju.88 continued its flight home and there was little indication of serious damage having been inflicted. Downhearted, the Beau crew returned to Coltishall.

In November 1988(!) Jeremy Howard-Williams learned that his shots *had* found their mark: the Ju.88 (Werk Nu.1479) of 3/Arklärungsgruppe 122 had sustained critical damage to the starboard engine and had forced-landed off the Dutch coast, 20 kilometres north of Alkmaar. Its crew of *Oberfeldwebel* Heinz Gunter Zabiensky (pilot), *Oberleutnant* Ludwig Blankenhahn (observer) and *Feldwebel* Rolf Lampmann (gunner) survived the encounter with minor wounds, though Zabiensky and Lampmann were destined not to survive the war.

On the night of 15/16 May, 1943, Dornier bombers of KG2, based at Soesterberg, Holland, launched an attack on Sunderland. The raid was officially described as 'heavy'. During the course of the attack the *Luftwaffe* lost one aircraft, which fell to the guns of a Beaufighter of 604 Squadron, Scorton.

The Dornier plunged into the sea some 30 miles east of Sunderland and it is not known whether any of the crew managed to bale out before impact. The pilot was 23-year-old *Unteroffizier* Karl Roos, whose body was washed up on the beach at Blackhall Rocks on 30 June, 1943.

The scene depicted is believed to be that of Roos' funeral at the Acklam Road cemetery, Thornaby, where the RAF had its own burial plot. As was the custom of the time, Roos was buried with full military honours. (Author's collection)

PARTING SHOT

SCARBOROUGH, 3/4 MARCH 1945

Leutnant Arnold Döring, 4/NJG3, shot down two four-engined bombers in the Dishforth-Topcliffe area on the night of 3/4 March, 1945. On the way out he decided to use his remaining ammunition on 'targets of opportunity'.

> *"We were not expected to return home with any ammunition left in our nose guns and we were free to attack any targets, on the ground or in the air. The Tommies did this in the day, shooting at vehicles, trains and men in fields, villages and towns. Now we would fight back and repay like for like. A light briefly illuminated a train travelling north, a long burst of my fire set fire to a wagon and the train let out a lot of steam as I shot it full of holes. I fired the last of my ammunition into the streets of the harbour town of Scarborough, jumped over the coast and out to sea. A searchlight illuminated a barrage balloon, which we were able to fly over, thanks to the Lord, and we went down to only a few metres above the sea and headed for home."*

Quoted by Simon Parry: *Intruders over Britain* Air Research Publications, 1987.

APPENDIX I

DETAILS OF GERMAN AIRCRAFT KNOWN TO HAVE CRASHED IN THE THREE NORTH-EAST COUNTIES OF BRITAIN OR WITHIN 25 MILES OF THEIR COASTLINE.

My own records of crashes of *Luftwaffe* aircraft and the demise of their crews have been supplemented by information from Ulf Balke: *Der Luftkrieg in Europa* vol 2. (Koblenz, 1990) and from W. G. Ramsay (ed): *The Blitz, then and now* vols 1-3 (After the Battle Publications, 1987-1990.)

NORTHUMBERLAND

Date	Type	Unit	Crash site	Cause
1939				
29 Nov	He.111	Stab/KG26	5miles E of Amble	111(Hurricane)Sqdn Acklington
1940				
30 Jan	He.111	4/KG26(1H+KM)	5miles E of Coquet Island	43(Hurricane)Sqdn, Acklington
3 Feb	He.111	3/KG26(1H+HL)	Druridge Bay, nr Amble	43(Hurricane)Sqdn, Acklington
3 Feb	He.111	2/KG26(1H+GK)	15miles E of Tynemouth	43(Hurricane)Sqdn, Acklington
27 Feb.	He.111	3/KG26	10miles E of Coquet Island	152(Spitfire)Sqdn, Acklington
29 Mar	Ju.88	6/KG30(4D+AP)	Cresswell Bay	Naval gunfire
27 Jun	He.111	2/KG4	Off Blyth	Unknown
*15 Aug	He.111	1/KG26	Cresswell Bay	72(Spitfire)Sqdn, Acklington;605(Hurricane)Sqdn, Drem
*15 Aug	Me.110	2/ZG76(M8+EK)	Off N'berland coast	following engagement by fighters. No other details known.
16 Sep	He.115 (3261)	Ku.Fl.Gr.3/ 506(S4+CL)	Ditched 7miles NE of Alnmouth	Naval gunfire (a/c towed to Eyemouth and beached)
1941				
14 Mar	Ju.88 (2234)	Ku.Fl.Gr.3/ 106(M2+JL)	In sea off Amble	Thought to be 72(Spitfire)Sqdn, Acklington
10 Apr	Ju.88 (0529)	3(F)/122(F6+NL)	Alnmouth	72(Spitfire)Sqdn, Acklington
30 Apr	Ju.88 (0715)	Ku.Fl.Gr.1/ 506(S4+JH)	Off Farne Islands	Thought to be 72(Spitfire)Sqdn, Acklington
6 May	He.111 (3520)	1/KG4(5J+IH)	Whorlton Park, nr Newcastle	Night-fighter; unit unknown
6 May	He.111 (3550)	2/KG53(A1+CK)	Morpeth	141(Defiant)Sqdn, Acklington
7 May	Ju.88 (7177)	5/KG30(4D+EN)	Holy Island	141(Defiant)Sqdn, Acklington
2 Jun	Ju.88 (3422)	Ku.Fl.Gr.3/ 106(M2+DL)	4miles NE of Newcastle	317(Hurricane)Sqdn, Ouston

23 Aug	He.111 (3691)	Stab/KG26 (1H+EA)	In sea N off Holy Island	Naval gunfire
1 Sep	Ju.88 (1064)	StabIII/KG30(4D+BD)	Bedlington brickworks	406(Beau.)Sqdn, Acklington
3 Oct	Do.217 (5309)	5/KG2(U5+GN)	6miles E of Blyth	406(Beau.)Sqdn, Acklington

1942

16 Jan	Ju.88 (1612)	Ku.Fl.Gr.1/506(S4+EH)	In sea off River Tyne	Anti-aircraft fire
15 Feb	Do.217 (1167)	StabIII/KG2(U5+BD)	4miles E of Blyth	141(Beau.)Sqdn, Acklington
15 Feb	Do.217 (5343)	9/KG2(U5+NT)	Off Blyth	Anti-aircraft fire
26 Mar	Do.217 (0063)	6/KG40(F8+KP)	20miles NE of Tynemouth	Anti-aircraft fire
19 Sep	Do.217 (4262)	7/KG2(U5+KR)	Off Tynemouth	219(Beau.)Sqdn, Acklington
20 Sep	Do.217 (4262)	7/KG2(U5+KR)	Off Tynemouth	219(Beau.)Sqdn, Acklington

1943

11 Mar	Ju.88 (144378)	9/KG6(3E+CT)	Off Blyth	Believed to be Beaufighter
13 Mar	Do.217 (4737)	7/KG2(U5+BD)	Off Tyne	219(Beau.)Sqdn, Scorton
25 Mar	Do.217 (5432)	3/KG2(U5+DL)	Madan Law, Kirknewton	Possibly hit by anti-aircraft fire before striking hill
25 Mar	Do.217 (1182)	7/KG2(U5+KR)	Twice Brewed, Haltwhistle	Struck hill
25 Mar	Ju.88 (144354)	1/KG6(3E+BH)	Linhope Rigg, nr Powburn	Struck hill
13 Mar	Do.217 (4737)	7/KG2(U5+BD)	Off Tyne	219(Beau.)Sqdn, Scorton
24 May	Do.217 (4268)	1/KG2(U5+HH)	Tynemouth	Thought to be 409(Beau.)Sqdn, Acklington

1940

1 Jul	He.59	Seenotflug Kdo.3(D-ASAM)	8miles east of Sunderland	72(Spitfire)Sqdn, Acklington
19 Jul	Fw.200	I/KG40(F8+EH)	Off shore east of Crimdon	Anti-aircraft fire
9 Aug	He.111	7/KG26(1H-ER)	Off Whitburn	79(Hurricane)Sqdn, Acklington
*15 Aug	Me.110	1/ZG76(M8+CH)	Streatlam, nr Barnard Castle	41(Spitfire)Sqdn, Catterick

*[SEE NOTE AT END OF TABLES]

5 Sep	He.111 (3065)	6/KG4(5J+JP)	Suffolk Street, Sunderland	Anti-aircraft fire
17 Nov	Ju.88 (0426)	3(F)/122(F6+HL)	Off shore east of Whitburn	Naval gunfire (paddle-driven minesweeper *Southsea*

1941

16 Feb	He.111 (3085)	6/KG4(5J+GP)	Bent's Park, South Shields	Anti-aircraft fire and collision with balloon cable
9 Dec	Ju.88 (1465)	3(F)/122(F6+CL)	10miles E of Seaham Harbour	Thought to be 43(Hurricane)Sqdn, Acklington

1942

8 Jul	Do.217 (4270)	9/KG2(U5+BT)	30miles E of Hartlepool	406(Beau.)Sqdn, Scorton
28 Aug	Ju.88 (144146)	StabI/KG77(3Z+CB)	In sea off Sunderland	406(Beau.)Sqdn, Scorton

1943

11 Mar	Do.217 (5441)	3/KG2(U5+BL)	Gt. Stainton, nr Darlington	219(Beau.)Sqdn, Scorton
16 May	Do.217 (4584)	6/KG2(U5+DP)	c.30miles off Sunderland	604(Beau.)Sqdn, Scorton

YORKSHIRE
1939

17 Oct	He.111	1(F)/122(F6+PK)	25miles E of Whitby	41(Spitfire)Sqdn, Catterick
21 Oct	He.115	Ku.Fl.Gr.1/406	5miles E of Spurn Head	46(Hurricane)Sqdn, Digby
10 Nov	Do.18 (0804)	Ku.Fl.Gr.3/406(K6+DL)	ENE of Scarborough	220(Hudson)Sqdn, Thornaby

1940

3 Feb	He.111 (2323)	4/KG26(1H+FM)	Bannial Flatt Farm, Whitby	43(Hurricane)Sqdn, Acklington
3 Apr	He.111	II/KG26(1H+AC)	15miles E of Redcar	41(Spitfire)Sqdn, Catterick
26 Jun	He.111	3/KG4(5J+BL)	Off Humber	Thought to be 616(Spitfire)Sqdn, Leconfield

1 Jul	He.111	3/KG4(5J+EL)	c.25miles E of Humber	616(Spitfire)Sqdn, Leconfield
1 Jul	He.115	Ku.Fl.Gr.3/106(M2+CL)	30miles E of Whitby	Engine failure
8 Jul	Ju.88	9/KG4(5J+AT)	Hornsea, nr Bridlington	41(Spitfire)Sqdn, Catterick. Also attacked by 249(Hurricane)Sqdn.
9 Jul	Ju.88	9/KG4	Hornsea	Unknown
11 Aug	Ju.88	1(F)/121(7A+KH)	Newton Moor, Scaling, Whitby	41(Spitfire)Sqdn, Catterick
*15 Aug	He.111	8/KG26(1H+FS)	30miles E of River Tees	Thought to be 605(Hurricane)Sqdn, Drem
*15 Aug	Ju.88	3/KG30(4D+KL)	Barmston, nr Bridlington	Attributed to 73(Hurricane)Sqdn, Church Fenton
*15 Aug	Ju.88	7/KG30(4D+DR)	Off A.165 c.4miles N of Bridlington	Attributed to 616(Spitfire)Sqdn, Leconfield
*15 Aug	Ju.88	4/KG30	Believed to be Flamboro' Head	Attributed to 73(Hurricane)Sqdn, Church Fenton

* [SEE NOTE AT END OF TABLES]

20 Aug	Ju.88	8/KG30(4D+IS)	Patrington, nr Hull	302(Hurricane)Sqdn, Leconfield
21 Aug	He.111 -H2	9/KG53(A1+T)	c.15 mls E Scarborough	P/O EA Shipman 41(Spitf.)Sqdn,Catterick
27 Oct	Ju.88 (6129)	7/KG4(5J+ER)	Duggleby, nr Malton	Ground fire from Searchlight Bty.
1 Nov	Ju.88	8/KG30(4D+TS)	Glaisdale Head, Whitby	Poor weather conditions

1941

30 Mar	Ju.88	1(F)/123(4U+GH)	Barnaby Moor, Tees-side	41(Spitf.)Sqdn,Catterick
16 Apr	He.111 (9370)	3/KG53(A1+AL)	Huby, nr York	Engine failure
5 May	Ju.88	6/KG77(3Z+FP)	In sea off Bridlington	Engine failure
8 May	He.111 (3987)	Stab1/KG4(5J+ZB)	Withernsea	Thought to be 151(Hurricane)Sqdn, Wittering
9 May	He.111 (4006)	4/KG53(A1+FM)	Patrington, nr Hull	255(Defiant)Sqdn, Kirton-in-Lindsey
9 May	He.111 (4042)	6/KG53(A1+CW)	Patrington, nr Hull	255(Defiant)Sqdn, Kirton-in-Lindsey
9 May	He.111 (3000)	6/KG55(G1+FP)	Long Riston, nr Beverley	255(Defiant)Sqdn, Kirton-in-Lindsey
15 May	Ju.88 (6263)	6/KG1(V4+GP)	Off Spurn Head	Naval gunfire(patrol boat *Protective*)
4 Jun	Ju.88 (0570)	2/NJG2(R4+LK)	Skelder Moor, nr Whitby	Thought to be bad visibility
10 Jul	Ju.88 (2227)	Ku.Fl.Gr.2/106(M2+EK)	Cliff Farm, Staithes	Struck cliffs in poor visibility
10 Jul	Ju.88 (4386)	Ku.Fl.Gr.2/106(M2+AL)	Speeton, nr Filey	Uncertain, though poor visibility possible cause

10 Jul	Ju.88 (3245)	Ku.Fl.Gr.2/106(M2+CL)	Speeton, nr Filey	Uncertain, though poor visibility possible cause
11 Jul	He.111 (3956)	8/KG4(5J+ES)	Off Humber	Unknown
10 Nov	Ju.88 (1409)	Ku.Fl.Gr.2/506(S4+HK)	Ravenscar, nr Whitby	Naval gunfire(HMS *Quantock*)

1942

15 Jan	Do.217 (5314)	8/KG2(U5+HS)	South Bank, Middlesbrough	Struck balloon cable
19 Jan	Ju.88 (0440)	3(F)122(F6+PL)	20 miles E of Whitby	Possibly 145(Spitf)Sqdn, Catterick
18 Feb	Do.217 (5342)	7/KG2(U5+KR)	Humber area	609(Spitf)Sqdn, Digby
27 Feb	Do.217 (1176)	9/KG2(U5+ST)	Humber area	Cause unknown
28 Feb	Do.217 (5436)	8/KG2(U5+AS)	Humber area	Naval gunfire; vessel unknown
9 Mar	Do.217 (5335)	9/KG2(U5+LT)	Humber area	Cause unknown
29 Apr	Do.217 (1164)	6/KG2(U5+KP)	Coneysthorpe, nr Malton	406(Beau.)Sqdn, Scorton
30 Apr	Ju.88 (1334)	Ku.Fl.Gr.1/106(M2+CH)	Elvington	Thought to be 253(Hurricane)Sqdn, Hibaldstow
8 Jul	Do.217 (5465)	4/KG2(U5+BM)	Off River Tees	406(Beau.)Sqdn, Scorton
8 Jul	Do.217 (4270)	9/KG2(U5+BT)	Off River Tees	406(Beau.)Sqdn, Scorton
6 Sep	Me.210 (2348)	16/KG6(2H+CA)	New Marske	1(Typhoon)Sqdn, Acklington
6 Sep	Me.210 (2321)	16/KG6(2H+HA)	Fylingthorpe, nr Robin Hood's Bay	1(Typhoon)Sqdn, Acklington
24 Sep	Do.217 (4294)	1/KG2(U5+FH)	off Flamboro Head	25(Beau.)Sqdn, Church Fenton
17 Dec	Do.217 (4342)	7/KG2(U5+GR)	Crow Nest, nr Helmsley	Anti-aircraft fire; forced landing in bad weather
17 Dec	Do.217 (5600)	2/KG2(U5+AK)	Ravenstones, Wheeldale Moor, nr Whitby	Anti-aircraft fire 17kms before crash

1943

4 Jan	Do.217 (4314)	9/KG2(U5+KT)	Skeffling, nr Withernsea	Anti-aircraft fire
16 Jan	Do.217 (4272)	9/KG2(U5+AT)	Humber area	Thought to be 25(Beau.) Sqdn, Church Fenton
4 Feb	Do.217 (5462)	3/KG2(U5+GL)	Muston, nr Filey	219(Beau.)Sqdn, Scorton
13 Jul	Do.217 (4479)	4/KG2(U5+EM)	c.10miles off Humber	410(Beau.)Sqdn, Coleby Grange
26 Jul	Do.217 (4412)	Stab/KG2(U5+BA)	15miles E Spurn Head	604(Beau.)Sqdn, Scorton
26 Jul	Do.217 (6045)	2/KG2(U5+GK)	Off Spurn Head	604(Beau.)Sqdn, Scorton

26 Jul	Do.217 (4395)	5/KG2(U5+AN)	Long Riston, nr Beverley	Anti-aircraft fire
22 Sep	Do.217 (4620)	4/KG2(U5+CM)	Out Newton, nr Withernsea	Crashed attempting to escape from searchlights
2 Oct	Ju.188 (260175)	2/KG66(Z6+GK)	½ml off Spurn Head lighthouse	Struck sea while taking evasive action

1945

| 4 Mar | Ju.88 (620028) | 13/NJG3(D5+AX) | Sutton-on-Derwent | Struck a tree while low flying |

*[15 Aug. 1940: Known as 'Black Thursday', the only time that the Luftwaffe launched a massed attack in *daylight* against the northern counties. They suffered heavily for it. Certainly more aircraft than those listed were shot down over the three counties and their coastal waters on that day. Some sources estimate totals of: 6 He.111s; 7 Me.110s; and 6 Ju.88s. The details, however, are confused and have thus been omitted.]

V-1 ROCKET ATTACKS

In addition to the crashes listed in the preceding pages, V-1 rockets also fell on County Durham and Yorkshire. Although they were flying *bombs*, it has been decided to include their crash sites in this volume.

Just after dawn on 24 December, 1944, 45 V-1 rockets were launched off the east coast by Heinkel 111s of III/KG53, each aircraft carrying one rocket. Their target was Manchester.

Thirty-one missiles crossed the coast but not all reached their designated target. Eight rockets fell in the counties of Durham and Yorkshire:

COUNTY DURHAM
Tudhoe, nr Spennymoor

YORKSHIRE
Grange Moor, Huddersfield
Midhope Moor, Penistone
Willerby, nr Hull
Barmby Moor, Pocklington
Rossington, nr Doncaster
Sowerby Bridge
South Cliffe, nr Market Weighton

A full account of the V-1 attacks on the north of England is given in Peter J. C. Smith's *The Christmas Eve Flying Bomb Raid on Manchester* [The Blitz, then and now. vol.3 pp 498-505. After the Battle Pub's 1990]

IN MESSAGE FORM

DATE	Time at which receipt or despatch of message was completed	Telephonist's Initials
6/9/42	1300.	Wm

ADDRESS TO :— Control Group 6

TEXT OF MESSAGE :—

Special Report

Supposed Junkers 88 brought down by gunfire 50 yards North of Redcar Water reservoir New Buildings. one German body recovered from reservoir. one parachute unopened 100 yds South of reservoir. Parachutist dead, tail of plane 200 yds north of orchard Cottage Hospital

Occurrence Number

TIME OF ORIGIN OF MESSAGE :— 1257

ADDRESS FROM :— Saltburn R/O.

The Messerschmitt 210 was a very rare visitor indeed to northern parts of England. When one crashed at New Marske most observers believed it to be a Junkers 88, but it is clear from the above message that one observer had his doubts. It is believed that the aircraft was the first Me. 210 to crash on English soil: most of the wreck was taken to Farnborough for evaluation. (See story on page 160)

APPENDIX II

LUFTWAFFE WAR GRAVES (CHEVINGTON, SUNDERLAND, THORNABY-ON-TEES, BRANDESBURTON)

At the cessation of hostilities in 1945, some 6,000 German dead of two world wars lay buried in municipal cemeteries and village churchyards in more than 700 different locations throughout Britain. The toll included those who had died in captivity, crew-members from World War I airships, dead who had been washed ashore and crews of crashed war planes.

In the late 1950s steps were taken to establish a German military cemetery on Cannock Chase (Staffs) to which all German war dead buried in Great Britain and Northern Ireland might ultimately be transferred. On 16 October, 1959, an agreement signed by the governments of Britain and the Federal Republic of Germany empowered the German War Graves Commission to take responsibility for the creation of the cemetery and the transfer of German war dead to it.

The first programme of re-burials occurred during 1962/63 and that was followed by a second during 1966/67. The consecration of the Cannock War Cemetery (*Deutschen Soldatenfriedhof*) took place on 10 July, 1967, when it was opened to the public. 4,939 German dead lie there: 2,143 from World War I and 2,796 from World War II.

However, not all have been transferred. In some instances relatives refused to grant permission for exhumation; in other cases, graves could not be opened because Germans had been interred in communal plots with British civilians. In cases where Germans had been buried in British War cemeteries, the authorities were reluctant to agree to removals if the effect would be to destroy the overall appearance of the British plots.

Thus, although most German war dead have now been transferred to Cannock, 263 from the 1914-18 war and 1,044 from the 1939-45 conflict still rest in the churchyards and cemeteries to which they were allocated some fifty or seventy years ago. It is believed that 954 of this number are *Luftwaffe* personnel who lost their lives in operations against this country during the Second World War.

The writer is aware of four sites in the north of England that have become the final resting places of a total of seventy *Luftwaffe* aircrew who failed to return home. The following gives the names of those men, their burial place, and a brief account of the circumstances leading to their demise.

Chevington cemetery, nr Broomhill, Northumberland

Date	Rank	Name	Aircraft	Code & Unit
1940				
3 Feb	Lt	Luther von Brüning	He.111	1H+HL;3/KG26
	Fw	Herbert Panzlaff		
	Uffz	Walter Remischke		

Shot down by 43(Hurricane)Sqdn, Acklington. Crashed in Druridge Bay. Fourth crew member Fw H. Peterson missing, believed killed.

27 Feb	Hptmn	Joachim Helm	He.111	?;2/KG26
	Uffz	Karl Lassnig		

Shot down by 152(Spitfire)Sqdn, Acklington. Crashed east of Coquet Island. Lassnig's body recovered on 1 March and that of Helm (*Staffelkapitan*) two days later. Other crew members – *Unteroffizier* Heinrich Buchisch; *Oberfeldwebel* Arthur Thiele; *Gefreiter* Walter Rixen – missing, believed killed.

29 Mar	Oblt	Rudolf Quadt	Ju.88	4D+AP;6/KG30
	Fw	Gustav Hartung		
	Uffz	Ernst Hesse		
	?	Andreas Wunderling		

Shot down by naval gunfire and crashed in Cresswell Bay.

1941				
1 Sep	Obfw	Helmut Riede	Ju.88	4D+BD
	Obfw	Helmut Dorn		StabIII/KG30
	Fw	Walter Muller		(Werk Nu.1064)
	Oblt	Rudolf Elle		

Crashed on Bedlington Station brickworks. Claimed by 406(Beaufighter)Squadron, Acklington.

1943				
25 Mar	Obfw	Friedrich Lang	Ju.88	3E+BH;1/KG6
	Obfw	Karl Klieh		(Werk Nu.144354)
	Gefr	Werner Fiedler		
	Uffz	Walter Schultz		

Crashed on Linhope Rigg, Powburn, while low-flying. One of three aircraft to crash in Northumberland in similar circumstances that night.

Castletown cemetery, Hylton, Sunderland

Date	Rank	Name	Aircraft	Unit & Code
1940				
5 Sep	Ogefr	Rudolf Marten	He.111	5J+JP;KG4
	Oblt	Hans W. Schroeder		(Werk Nu.3065)
	Uffz	Fritz Reitz		
	Gefr	Josef Wich		

Shot down by AA fire during a night attack on Sunderland. Crashed behind Suffolk Street, Hendon.

1941				
16 Feb	Obfw	Wilhelm Beetz	He.111	5J+GP;KG4
	Gefr	Franz Janeschitz		(Werk Nu.3085)
	Uffz	Helmut Jeckstadt		
	Uffz	Karl Brutzen		

Hit by AA fire then struck a balloon cable. Crashed at Bent's Park, South Shields. Beetz baled out but was killed when he landed on trolley-bus wires. Fifth crew member *Hauptmann* H. Styra missing, believed killed.

1942				
16 Jan	Lt	Dieter Andresen	Ju.88	S4+EH;
				Ku.Fl.Gr 1/506
				(Werk Nu.1612)

Shot down by AA fire and crashed in sea off the Tyne. Andresen's body was washed ashore on 27 January. Other crew members were *Feldwebel* F. Gruschka; *Unteroffizier* J. Scholze; *Unteroffizier* F. Pett. All missing, presumed killed. Possible that one is interred in the grave marked simply *'Ein Deutsche Soldat'*.

Acklam Road cemetery, Thornaby-on-Tees

Date	Rank	Name	Aircraft	Unit & Code
1940				
1 Nov	Fw	Wilhelm Wowereit	Ju.88	4D+TS;8/KG30
	Obfw	Hans Schulte-Mater		(Werk Nu.7089)
	Uffz	Alfred Rodermond		
	Uffz	Gerhard Pohling		

Struck hillside at Glaisdale Head, nr Whitby, c.5.00pm while *en route* to attack Linton-on-Ouse aerodrome. Precise cause unknown, though poor visibility suspected (eye-witnesses claim it was foggy).

1941				
30 Mar	Uffz	Hans Steigerwald	Ju.88	4U+GH;1(F)/123
				(Werk Nu.0115)

Was on an armed photo-reconnaissance sortie to Manchester when it was intercepted over south Durham by two Spitfires of 41 Sqdn, Catterick. It was shot down by ex-Ampleforth schoolboy F/Lt Tony Lovell and crashed on Eston Hills, Tees-side, at 3.15pm. Other crew members − *Leutnant* Wolfgang Schlott; *Leutnant* Otto Meingold; *Feldwebel* Wilhelm Schmigale − were obliterated with their aircraft when its bomb load exploded on impact. Steigerwald baled out but his parachute 'Roman-candled' and he fell among the trees that line Flatts Lane, Normanby. (See main text: 'A Ju.88 crashes')

27 Apr	Oblt	Hildebrand	Ju.88	M2+JL
		Voigtländer-Tetzner		Ku.Fl.Gr 3/106
				(Werk Nu.2234)

Crashed into the sea off Amble, Northumberland, 14 March. Possibly shot down by a Spitfire of 72 Sqdn, Acklington. On 27 April Voigtländer-Tetzner's body was recovered from the sea, one mile south-east of the Heugh Light, Hartlepool. He was therefore buried under that date. Other crew members − *Leutnant* Rudolf Dietze; *Obergefreiter* Walter Wesserer; *Obergefreiter* Hans Vandamme − missing, believed killed.

4 Jun	Lt	Johannes Feuerbaum	Ju.88	R4+LK;2/NJG2
	Gefr	Gerhard Denzin		(Werk Nu.0570)
	Gefr	Rudolf Peters		

Was on night intruder operations and had just crossed in near Whitby when it crashed on Skelder Moor in conditions of poor visibility.

10 Jul	Oblt	Edgar Peisart	Ju.88	M2+EK;
	Lt	Rudolf Bellof		Ku.Fl.Gr 2/106
	Gefr	Gerhard Vogel		(Werk Nu.2227)
	Fw	Karl Kinder		

One of three aircraft briefed to carry out anti-shipping patrols between Holy Island and Whitby. Peisart reached his patrol line but encountered mist and flew into cliffs below Cliff Farm, Staithes, at 00.06am. The other two aircraft suffered a similar fate: they crashed at Speeton, nr Filey, in misty conditions. (See main text: 'Encounters with Cliffs')

10 Nov	Obfhr	Karl Schultze	Ju.88	S4+HK;
	Obfw	Werner Hanel		Ku.Fl.Gr 2/506
				(Werk Nu.1408)

Shot down by HMS *Quantock* while attacking a convoy off Ravenscar, nr Whitby. Crashed just off shore at Blea Wyke Point at c.5.30pm. Other crew members – *Oberleutnant* Heinz Weber *(Staffelkapitan)* and *Unteroffizier* Arthur Graber – missing. It is believed that these crew members are buried in the two graves marked *'Ein Deutsche Soldat'*.

1942

15 Jan	Fw	Joachim Lehnis	Do.217	U5+HS; 8/KG2
	Lt	Rudolf Matern		(Werk Nu.5314)
	Obfw	Heinrich Richter		

Collided with barrage balloon cable and crashed into a coal yard in Clay Lane, South Bank, Middlesbrough, at 6.05pm. May well be that this aircraft had earlier attacked Skinningrove Ironworks and had bombed the SS *Empire Bay* (which later sank off the Tees) before its own demise. Fourth member of the crew, Hans Maneke, missing. (See main text: '"Annie" snares a German bomber')

31 Aug	Obfw	Paul Kolodzie	Ju.88	3Z+CB; 3/KG77
	Gefr	Josef Sanden		(Werk Nu.0144146)

Shot down off Sunderland on 28 August by 406 (Beau) Sqdn, Scorton. Kolodzie's body was retrieved from the sea off Crimdon Dean; Sanden's from Blackhall Rocks. Two other crew members, *Oberfeldwebel* Alfred Reidel and *Feldwebel* Josef Pfeffer, baled out and were captured. The Beaufighter crashed on its return to Scorton and its crew of two were killed.

6 Sep	Fw	Heinrich Mösges	Me.210	2H+CA; 16/KG6
	Ogefr	Eduard Czerny		(Werk Nu.173)

One of a pair believed to have been on armed reconnaissance when intercepted over the Tees by two Typhoons of 1 Sqdn, Acklington. Shot down by P/O Perrin and crashed at Fell Briggs Farm, New Marske at c.11.45am. The crew baled out but neither parachute opened. The second Me.210 was pursued as far as Robin Hood's Bay before it was shot down by Perrin's No.2 P/O Bridges. The crew baled out and were made POWs. (See main text: 'Duel over New Marske')

17 Dec	Fw	Wilhelm Stoll	Do.217	U5+AK; 2/KG2
	Ogefr	Hans Roeschner		(Werk Nu.5600)
	Ogefr	Gerhard Wicht		
	Ogefr	Franz Armann		

Crashed at Ravenstones, Wheeldale Moor, Goathland, *while en route* to attack York. It is thought that it was hit by AA fire some 15 miles east of the crash site. It then went through some bad weather before striking the hillside. The same evening a second Do.217 (of 7/KG2) en route to York crashed into the hillside at Crow Nest, nr Hawnby, some 6 miles north-west of Helmsley.

1943

| 30 Jun | Uffz | Karl Roos | Do.217 | U5+DP; 6/KG2 |
| | | | | (Werk Nu.4584) |

Shot down 35 miles east of Sunderland by 604(Beau) Sqdn, Scorton, on 16 May. Roos' body was washed ashore at Blackhall Rocks on 30 June and he was buried under that date. Other crew members – *Obergefreiter* Gunter Kaeber; *Unteroffizier* Bruno Mittlestadt; *Unteroffizier* Alfred Richter – missing.

Brandesburton churchyard, nr Hornsea, East Yorkshire

Date	Rank	Name	Aircraft	Unit & Code
1941				
8 May	Obfw	Alfred Hoffman	He.111	5J+ZB; StabI/KG4

Crash-landed on Withernsea beach. Possibly shot down by 151(Hurricane) Sqdn, Wittering. Of the other crew members, *Oberleutnant zur See* P. Tholen and *Oberfeldwebel* H. Schroder were captured; *Feldwebel* W. Schrieber was killed (burial place unknown).

Date	Rank	Name	Aircraft	Unit & Code
9 May	Gefr	Hans Steiglitz	He.111	A1+CW; 6/KG53
	Gefr	Johannes Kaminski		(Werk Nu. 4042)
	Gefr	Willi London		
	Gefr	Herman Decker		

Crashed at Patrington, nr Hull, having been shot down by 255(Defiant) Sqdn, Kirton-in-Lindsey. Crew member *Unteroffizier* H. Teschke baled out and was captured.

Date	Rank	Name	Aircraft	Unit & Code
9 May	Uffz	Gunter Reinelt*	He.111	A1+FM; 4/KG53
	Uffz	Jacob Kalle		(Werk Nu.4006)
	Ogefr	Rudolf Lorenz		

Crashed at Patrington, nr Hull, after being attacked by a Defiant of 255 Sqdn, Kirton-in-Lindsey. Crew member *Unteroffizier* F. Magie baled out and was captured; *Gefreiter* H. Wulf missing. (*date on headstone is given as 10 May, 1941)

Date	Rank	Name	Aircraft	Unit & Code
10 May	Ogefr	Josef Schumacher	Ju.88	S4+JH;
				Ku.Fl.Gr 1/506
				(Werk Nu. 0715

Crashed off Farne Islands, Northumberland, on 1 May. Schumacher's body recovered from the sea and landed at a nearby port. Burial place of other crew members — *Leutnant* H. Jark; *Feldwebel* K. Pahneke; *Unteroffizier* J. Schaare — unknown.

1943

Date	Rank	Name	Aircraft	Unit & Code
26 Jul	Ogefr	Rudolf Trodler	Do.217	U5+AN; 5/KG2
	Uffz	Fritz Pilger		(Werk Nu. 4395)
	Uffz	Hans Ulrich Cowle		
	Uffz	Helmut Gabriel		

Crashed at Long Riston, nr Beverley, after being hit by AA fire.

APPENDIX III

MIDDLESBROUGH AND EAST CLEVELAND: CHRONICLE OF KNOWN AIR RAIDS, 1940-1943

(**raids dealt with more fully in the main text)

KEY: HE = high-explosives; IBs = incendiaries

During the Second World War Middlesbrough suffered 481 alerts and twelve air raids. 135 high-explosives fell within the borough boundary and hundreds of incendiary bombs were dropped by raiding aircraft on twelve separate occasions; seventy-eight of its citizens were killed, 172 seriously injured and 422 slightly injured; 318 buildings were destroyed and a further 8,547 others suffered varying degrees of damage. Although the town was more fortunate than might have been expected at the outbreak of war in 1939, the final cost was nevertheless a high price to pay for international madness.

At the time, the Air Raids Precautions (ARP) Committee compiled records of each attack, but it would seem that not all files have survived to the present day. However, those that the writer has managed to locate (including some which relate to the wider Cleveland area) have been included in chronological sequence in the following pages.

1940

25 May, 1940**
0141-1235hrs. Fourteen small calibre HE fell in a line which stretched from Cargo Fleet Ironworks, South Bank, to Dorman, Long's south steel plant, Grangetown. Negligible industrial damage was caused but there was structural damage to housing in Aire Street, South Bank. There were eight casualties (three needing hospitalization) among workmen at the Grangetown Works. This was the first air raid on an industrial target during the Second World War and it produced the first civilian casualties to arise from a bombing raid over England during the 1939-45 period.

6 June, 1940
0001-0052hrs. A German aircraft showing its navigation lights joined the circuit over Thornaby aerodrome while British planes were having night-bombing practice with all aerodrome lights exposed. The raider dropped 16 HE (each of c.50kg). Twelve fell in a straight line across the aerodrome, parallel to the hangars. Two Hudson aircraft (N7309; P5157) of No.220 Squadron were destroyed, a petrol tanker was covered with splinters and the north-south runway was damaged but not rendered unserviceable. Airman F. W. Nutter died of injuries the next day. In addition, two Sappers and one Gunner were wounded. The defenders fired six rounds at the raider but without success.

19/20 June, 1940
2310-0350hrs. There was intense air activity over the north-east generally before the Tees-side warning was sounded and relays of hostile aircraft passed over the area on their way inland. Enemy activity occurred at 2312hrs when 2 HE fell on Dorman's Acklam Wharf, causing damage to the wharf and to the steamship *Beeta*, which was lying alongside. The ship's gunner, a Royal Marine, was killed and the Third Engineer was blown overboard; eight workmen were wounded (one seriously). Two HE fell on the slag bank at Gjers Mills Ayresome Works, causing only slight damage to office windows, a weigh-cabin and a joiner's shop. Production was unaffected in both cases. During the raid an AA shell fell through the roof of 59 Warren Street and went through the bed on its way to the floor below. Fortunately, the occupants of the house were in the shelter.

26/27 June, 1940
2344-c.0050hrs. At 0030hrs an enemy aircraft dropped nine HE in a rough line that stretched from ICI Cassel Works (Billingham) to Middlesbrough Town Hall corner. It was in this attack that the car of the Transporter Bridge was struck and St Peter's Church, Feversham Street, was wrecked. There were no casualties.

25 August, 1940
0034-c.0200hrs. Fourteen HE were dropped at 0145hrs but some of these failed to explode. One UXB was found at the junction of Marton Burn Road/Beauville Road; another in City Road; one HE exploded at the junction of Thorndyke Avenue/Beechwood Avenue and caused damage to water and gas mains; another produced a similar result at the junction of Marton Burn Road/Kieth Road; two HE dropped near Beechwood Schools and allotments behind Thorndyke Avenue without apparent effect; the bomb that burst in West Lane (Newport end) caused very slight damage to housing and one minor casualty; one UXB was found buried in the Sutton Trust playing fields; property in Oswald Terrace suffered some minor damage when one HE landed there; one HE fell on the greyhound track and caused injury to a member of the barrage balloon crew posted there; one HE in Cannon Street caused slight damage to property; one HE at the junction of Connaught Road/Dunstable Road caused some damage; two HE landed on the railway sidings at Newport and caused some damage to lines and wagons.

28 August, 1940
0222-0330hrs. The attack occurred at 0314hrs. One HE fell on Meadowfield Avenue and two HE in The Vale. These bombs caused considerable damage to fourteen houses and resulted in the town's first air-raid death (Mrs Morley, 25 Meadowfield Avenue, Grove Hill). Nine others were treated for minor wounds and shock. Single UXBs were reported as having fallen behind Lawson Street Schools, Cargo Fleet, and between Holgate Hospital and the Special School.

28/29 August, 1940
2200-0148hrs. Four HE were dropped to the south of Middlesbrough and caused neither damage nor casualties: three of them fell on the north side of Ladgate Lane; the fourth fell on the south side of Tollesby Hall grounds. They made a straight line of craters, each 300ft from the next and each 30ft wide and 15ft deep.

18 September, 1940
2042-2144hrs. The attack took place at 2118hrs when a mine* was dropped at Bamlett's Bight, off Furness shipyard. It failed to explode. (*ARP records refer to it as magnetic, but it was probably a land mine.)

21 September, 1940
2134-2359hrs. Attack occurred at 2345hrs when one HE fell on a slag heap near Cargo Fleet Ironworks. Window damage affected c.200 houses in the Cargo Fleet/South Bank area. Two persons were injured by flying glass.

26 September, 1940
1100-1124hrs. An aircraft attacked Skinningrove Ironworks at c.1100hrs when four HE were dropped. Three men were injured and hospitalized; eight other persons were slightly injured. The scale of the damage incurred is not known.
1300hrs. One enemy aircraft circled over Loftus and was fired on by ground defences. No bombs were dropped.

13 October, 1940**
1936-2045hrs. Four HE fell in the Marsh Road area and caused a large number of casualties and severe damage to housing in the Benjamin Street/Hatherley Street district. Casualties numbered twenty killed and 105 injured (including thirty-two seriously).

1 November, 1940
0647-0719hrs. At c.0700hrs one enemy aircraft dropped seven HE which straddled the A.171 at Seldom Seen, nr Keld House Farm/Town House Farm, causing slight damage to allotment property. The same aircraft dropped five HE in fields belonging to Low Bottoms Farm, between Cargo Fleet Lane and Skippers Lane.

6 November, 1940
1757-1800hrs. One enemy aircraft dropped six small-calibre HE to the left of the Marske/Saltburn road, on the Saltburn side of Marske railway bridge, at 1758hrs. It subsequently dropped five light HE on Kilton Mill bank, nr Loftus, causing the death of a 19-year-old male when cottage property was damaged in the Kilton Mill bank area; a further person was injured.

9 November, 1940
0700-0939hrs. A number of HE were dropped on Whitby, but their effects are not known.
c.1842hrs. Three HE were dropped in the sea due north of Cliff House, Marske.

15/16 February, 1941

c.0220 hrs. Four HE fell on the Bridgeford Terrace/Middlesbrough Road area of South Bank. Seven houses were totally destroyed and five required demolition; there was serious damage to a further nine properties and slight damage to seventy-six others. Both Middlesbrough Road and Coral Street were blocked by debris. The search of the debris by would-be rescuers continued until 20th February, when the final casualty total was determined: twelve persons killed and twelve slightly injured.

15 March, 1941

0448hrs. Three HE fell on Chapel Bank, Loftus, so badly damaging the Wesleyan Chapel there that it had to be demolished. A further two HE dropped in nearby fields. Although these explosions caused damage to windows over a large area there were no casualties. IBs fell in fields at Easington, without apparent effect.

7/8 April, 1941

2045-0447hrs. At c.0012hrs two HE fell close to the junction of Pallister Avenue/Marshall Avenue, Brambles Farm. Four houses were completely demolished and three people were trapped under debris. Vera Morris (20 yrs) was found to be dead when released at 0400hrs. Ten people were slightly injured during the attack.

IBs were dropped on Normanby Ironworks, the west end of Cargo Fleet Ironworks, Boyd Estate, and Pine Street, Cargo Fleet. King's Road Methodist chapel, North Ormseby, was opened as a Rest Centre for the Brambles Farm incident and people were transferred there by bus ordered by ARP Control.

Across the river, parachute mines fell on Graythorpe village, nr Hartlepool, and wrecked fifty houses. One UXB (a parachute mine) resulted in the evacuation of the whole village.

15/16 April, 1941

2245-0458hrs. Gunfire commenced at 2250hrs and was intermittent for some hours. One parachute mine fell at Dorman, Long Britannia Works, smashing windows over a ¼-mile radius (over 800 in the Works alone) and putting shrapnel through 500 cast-iron sheets. One person was killed and three injured at the Construction Works. One parachute mine fell at Gjers Mill Works and caused slight damage to the wharf and slightly injured two persons.

c.0200hrs: two parachute mines were dropped on Thornaby: one on a derelict works and one in the Union Foundry. Industrial buildings (involving three firms) were seriously damaged and 140 houses were slightly damaged. One woman 'died from shock'; one man was seriously injured; and three women were slightly injured.

c.0410hrs: two parachute mines were dropped close by Loftus station footbridge. There was extensive damage to windows and roofs in the vicinity of Church Row and Loftus Cottages. Fourteen people were slightly injured.

19/20 April, 1941

Time unknown. Bombs were dropped at Whitby without effective result. It is thought that the raider was perhaps on anti-shipping patrol.

25/26 April, 1941

Time unknown. Bombs fell in Whitby; results unknown.

3 May, 1941

0249-0344hrs. On this night twenty aircraft were detailed to bomb the Hartlepools with thirty-two tonnes of HE and 2160 IBs. The concentration point of the attack was a 12-kilometre stretch between Hartlepool and West Hartlepool, where the docks and industrial installations were situated.

0300hrs. Three small delayed-action bombs fell on Dent's Wharf, Middlesbrough: one exploded on a warehouse filled with sisal and caused a 'very large fire of a highly inflammable character.'

At 0315hrs it was reported that '…at least one of the raiders was firing tracer bullets — presumably at barrage balloons.'

6/7 May, 1941

2318-0439hrs. The attack commenced at 0013hrs, when 100 IBs fell on Normanby Ironworks and one HE dropped in the river close by. Other IBs were dropped on the Tees Graving Dock (nine), Gjers Ayresome Ironworks (forty), Acklam Ironworks (200) and Dorman, Long's Britannia Works (six). There was minor damage to coke ovens and an office roof at the Ayresome plant and negligible IB damage elsewhere, although five workers were injured (one seriously) at Acklam Ironworks. One HE fell in Belle View Grove, Grove Hill, and caused extensive damage to fifty-five houses in Stanhope Gardens, Belle View Grove and Lansdowne Road; forty other properties in Belle View Grove suffered slight damage. Casualties were few: three males and six females suffered slight injuries. One HE exploded alongside the nearby railway line, seemingly without effect.

During the same night. One HE fell on the 14th green at Warrenby golf links and made a crater 50ft by 20ft some 200 yards from Warrenby School. One HE exploded on Redcar rocks and caused severe damage to windows along the esplanade. At South Bank, 'several HE fell in the Nelson Street/North Street/Napier Street area and gas-holders were hit and set on fire.'

7 May, 1941

1730hrs. c.200 IBs — including two oil bombs — fell between Grangetown's Police Court and railway station. The guard-room of the local AA Battalion was burned out, but it is not known whether casualties were inflicted.

8 May, 1941

0144-0330hrs. The Germans claimed that during the night of 7/8 May docks and industrial installations were bombed at Hartlepool (five aircraft), West Hartlepool (nine aircraft), and Middlesbrough and ICI Billingham (five aircraft). Some 200 IBs fell on central Middlesbrough, but most were quickly extinguished. A number of small fires affected shops and business premises and the Town Hall roof was damaged by an IB. A string of HEs was dropped on the town from north to south: one in the vicinity of Southfield Road/Marton Road; one in the yard of 79 Shakespeare Street; one in Albert park, opposite the fire station, and another opposite the maternity home; one in the grounds of the maternity hospital and one in its clinic; one in the vicinity of Hymas Street/Pierson Street, North Ormesby. Amazingly, *all* of these bombs failed to explode! Other explosives fell in open country near Loftus (one) and Little Ayton (one parachute mine). One HE fell at Tod Point, Warrenby, killing one person, and a number of IBs fell in Corporation Road, Redcar, without any known effect.

11/12 May, 1941

2352-0333hrs. The attack occurred at 0033hrs, when the first of seven HE and 'numerous' IBs dropped on Middlesbrough. One HE in the Glebe Road/St. Paul's area caused considerable damage to 150 houses and slight damage to 300 more; twenty-one people were injured, of whom seven required hospitalization, and 24-year-old Margaret Haswell was found to be dead on removal from the wreckage. Four HE fell at the corner of Linthorpe Road/Park Road South, causing damage to the Park Hotel. Two HE dropped on Ayresome Ironworks and caused sufficient damage to ensure that 'pig-iron production would be stopped for 6-8 weeks.' A number of IBs were dropped, but most of these fell in Linthorpe cemetery. On the same night five HE fell near Ladgates Farm, Brotton, and two HE dropped behind the Sun Street Corporation depot, Thornaby: neither of these attacks caused casualties.

16 May, 1941

0240-0434hrs. Six HE and a number of IBs fell on the town. One fell in Queen Mary Street, close to a gas-holder and a shelter, damaging the latter and causing minor injuries to two women and three children who were inside; at 0247hrs one HE exploded inside one of the Newport gas-holders, perforating it in numerous places and starting a spectacular fire; one HE fell near Foxheads Bridge; another dropped on the railway sidings leading to the works of Richard Hill & Co.; one dropped on waste ground in Depot Road and another on the railway siding near Acklam Works. On the same night, six HE fell on Eston slag tip.

11 July, 1941

0116-0300hrs. Two HE fell on the marshes on the south side of Redcar Wharf, causing neither damage nor casualties.

25 July, 1941

c.0125hrs. One HE and one UXB fell some 250 yards from No.5 blast-furnace, Skinningrove ironworks. One HE also dropped near Low Farm, Brotton. In neither case were damage or casualties inflicted.

19 August, 1941

0117-0336hrs. Intermittent bombing started in the Tees-side area at 0130hrs, when one HE fell on Redcar beach, close to the Coatham Hotel; another fell on Machine Lane, North Skelton, where it made a crater 40ft wide and 40ft deep; one HE fell at the pit head of the North Skelton mine. All of these bombs caused nothing more than broken windows in their respective districts. At 0230hrs one HE fell on the Acklam Works slag tip and another fell on the slag plant, the latter causing three casualties and extensive damage which threatened to reduce production by one-third; three HE dropped in the Tees, between Acklam Works and Britannia Works; at 0137hrs 'big fires' were observed in the direction of the ICI Synthetic plant, Billingham.

2318-2350hrs. At 2310hrs one HE fell on Gjers' tip to the north of Grangetown station and five HE dropped close by on the Teesport foreshore. No casualties or damage reported.

7 September, 1941

c.2230hrs. Five HE were dropped on Skinningrove Ironworks, causing minor injuries to seven males and slight damage to buildings. Four HE fell in Wiley Cot Wood, killing one cow and damaging the Water Company pump-house. One HE fell in Tocketts Wood but inflicted no damage.

11 September, 1941

2030hrs. Two HE fell near the No.2 coke oven at Skinningrove Works. One man (A. J. Carter, Loftus) was killed and five were injured. Slight damage was caused to the plant but there was no interference with production.

30 September, 1941

2059-2259hrs. Bombs were dropped over East Cleveland c.2200hrs. Two HE fell in Loftus, close to the United Bus Co. garage and the railway, badly damaging three houses and causing slight damage to a further thirty. There were eight casualties, including one requiring hospitalization. Two HE fell in the Guisborough district ("half a mile from a reservoir") but no damage was caused.

2 October, 1941

1956-2233hrs. A minor raid on the area occurred at 2125hrs when two HE fell on Gray's shipyard, Seaton Channel, South Bank, but caused no damage. One HE exploded at the back of Coral Street/Pearl Street, South Bank, demolishing a surface shelter and causing extensive damage to six houses at the west end of Pearl Street. Three persons were killed in the shelter: Charles Weston, Coral Street; Patrick McGee (aged 10½) and Kathleen McGee (aged 4); fourteen others were injured, three of whom were in the shelter. Four HE fell in the vicinity of Harcourt Road, while three UXBs were later located in fields between Eston Cemetery and Church Lane.

21 October, 1941**

2020-2250hrs. Bombs were dropped at a number of points throughout Cleveland in an attack which began at 2115hrs. One UXB fell on Gray's shipyard and another dropped in the Tees near the Malleable Wharf, Stockton; four HE fell at Gribdale Gate, Great Ayton; four HE nr Nunthorpe Church; four HE in Coal Pit field, Stanghow Lane, Skelton; four HE nr Priestcroft's Farm, Lingdale; two HE nr East Pastures Farm, Skelton; and two HE on the Whitby road, nr Easington. In the Redcar area, one bomb dropped on the golf course and another in a field close by; four HE landed in fields of West Coatham Grange Farm; one HE demolished 46 Queen Street and one struck the Zetland Club, Coatham Road. Most of the bombs caused no damage to life or property, but there was considerable minor damage to property in the Lingdale/Skelton area. Redcar suffered the most: the Zetland Club and surrounding properties were demolished. Fifteen people were killed and sixteen injured, including eight requiring hospitalization.

4 November, 1941

0422-0507hrs. One HE was dropped on the slag tip at the end of Miles Street/Codd Street, South Bank, at 0438hrs and made eleven houses temporarily uninhabitable and caused slight damage to 140 others. Seventy-six year-old Elizabeth Gibson, Alexander Hotel, was severely shocked and W. Bradley slightly injured. One x 500kg UXB (a suspected delayed-action device) was removed from the blacksmith shop at Warrenby Ironworks.

7 November, 1941

c.2210hrs. A number of HEs were widely scattered across Cleveland: three HE in the river at Teesport; four HE near Fox Rush Farm, Redcar; one HE and one UXB on the beach close to Hawthorn road, Redcar; one HE at Grewgrass Farm, New Marske; two HE on the Brotton coast road and four HE off Saltburn Lane, Skelton; one HE at Dinnerdown Hill, Loftus, and "a number of HEs in fields at East Loftus"; one HE nr Scaling Hill Farm; IBs at Ings Farm, Easington; and one HE in the grounds of Grinkle Hall. One person was slightly injured in the Loftus area and there was minor damage to property in the New Marske/Skelton areas.

10 November, 1941

1410-1415hrs. At 1411hrs Skinningrove Ironworks was bombed and machine-gunned by a single raider. Two HE fell on the railway to the west of the Talbot furnace, making craters 30ft across and 20ft deep and causing some damage to the track and slight damage to buildings. Six persons suffered minor injuries.

15 November, 1941

0927-0950hrs. A single aircraft dive-bombed Warrenby Ironworks at 0927hrs while the sirens were sounding. Two HEs were released and both ricochetted on hitting the ground. One exploded close to No.4 blast-furnace and the other burst 25 yards away. Nine persons were killed and seventeen hospitalized (including one who subsequently died); thirty-two others suffered less serious injuries. The main damage was to the gas cleaning plant and resulted in a temporary reduction in the output of pig-iron. Further damage was caused at 1025hrs and at 1125hrs due to gas explosions.

29 December, 1941

2020-2229hrs. At 2120hrs four HE exploded in a field 100 yards south-east of the Isolation Hospital, Flatts Lane, Normanby, causing neither damage nor casualties.

1942

13 January, 1942

1509-1547hrs. A single raider dropped four HE on Warrenby Works in a low-level attack which was delivered as the sirens were sounding. Ten persons were killed and five hospitalized; twenty-three others were less seriously injured. Slight damage to mill boilers caused two days' lost production.

26 March, 1942

2046-2211hrs. Four HE (each 500kg) were dropped in the fields of Hemlington Hall Farm, between the Bluebell corner and Stainton, at 2140hrs. Their precise effects are not known but it is believed that no serious damage resulted. Sunderland and Hull were the main targets that night.

15/16 April, 1942

2237-0123hrs. Aircraft attacked at 2346hrs when four HE fell in a line across Carlow Street, Mills Street and Laws Street and Newport recreation ground; four HE also fell in the river. The first stick of bombs produced major casualties: twenty-eight killed and thirty-nine injured. Damage to property was widespread: thirty-nine houses were rendered uninhabitable, 1,707 others were less seriously affected and 1,156 people were rendered homeless. Seven HE and two UXB fell in the Saltburn area, including one bomb which exploded between an empty shelter in Station Street and housing in Exeter Street. The shelter was destroyed and four properties required demolition. Casualties were one killed and eleven injured.

In the Marske area, four HE produced only minor damage. Seven HE and one UXB fell around New Marske, and four of these caused severe destruction at Sparrow Farm. Two HE fell in the Guisborough area to no effect. Eight HE dropped in open country around Loftus; ten HE in open areas in the Barnes Farm/Warren Wood/Mutton Scalp Lane district of Skelton; and ten HE in open areas around Redcar. Sunderland was the main target.

5 June, 1942

0118-0318hrs. Flares settled over Middlesbrough at 0148hrs. Shortly afterwards, IBs dropped in Cranfield Avenue/Marshall Avenue, Brambles Farm, where fires started at 0155hrs but caused only slight damage and no casualties. Bombs were scattered widely over Cleveland: four HE fell on Red Ghyll and four HE on Laurel Road, Saltburn, where three houses were demolished, forty others seriously damaged and 100 others being affected to a minor degree; 1,300 IBs were dropped over the Saltburn/Dormanstown district; four HE fell in Church Lane, Marske (where the vicarage was seriously affected and fourteen domestic properties suffered minor damage), and two HE on the beach; one UXB was discovered on the Marske/Redcar boundary; four HE fell harmlessly into the sea, "near the Orange gun-site"; three HE dropped on Lazenby marshes; IBs showered over Cleveland Ironworks, South Bank, and a short distance away two UXBs were found at St Peter's school; one HE landed in Normanby and four HE dropped on the Flatt's Lane brickworks, causing no casualties and only minor damage; four HE fell on open land nr the Trunk Road; three HE landed 'on the decoy airfield at Greatham' and three HE dropped on the nearby Gray's shipyard, seemingly to little effect; IBs also fell over Great Ayton and in the region of Danby Beacon. Given the numbers of bombs that were dropped, the area escaped very lightly. Total casualties amounted to five killed and seven injured, including a 15-year-old Dormanstown boy who was seriously injured when he handled an IB. Sunderland was the main target.

7 July, 1942

c.0140hrs. IBs were dropped over a wide area of Middlesbrough, including Linthorpe Road, Pelham Street, Portman Street, Percy Street, Victoria Road, Temple Street, Eldon Street, King Edward's Road, Clarendon Road, Amber Street, Garner Street, Ruby Street, and the Newport Ironworks. A number of fires were started: some were small and were extinguished by fire-watchers, but thirty-seven were serious enough to require attendance by the Fir Brigade, including seven fires rated as 'large'. Three churches – All Saints', St Aidan's, and St George's Congregational – sustained fire damage, and Middlesbrough High School was also affected.

8 July, 1942

0107-0228hrs. Flares appeared over Middlesbrough at 0130hrs and bombs started to fall at 0155hrs. One HE struck Billingham Reach wharf and damaged cranes and the canteen located there. Four HE caused slight damage to Dorman, Long Britannia Works, while HE that fell in the river damaged a nearby pump-house in addition to producing generalized effects due to shrapnel. One HE at Richard Hill's Wire Works resulted in the extensive destruction of galvanizing and fabrication workshops and also affected the No.2 barrage balloon site close by, where several persons were injured (one hospitalized). HE to the north of the Gjers Mills plant produced splinter damage which included the perforation and the sinking of the sand barge *Sweep*. Two HE on the works of Richardson, Westgarth demolished the engine-house, damaged the wharf and destroyed twenty motor-lorry chassis which were awaiting shipment. Dent's wharf was affected by five HE which damaged railway sidings, a joiner's shop and a balloon site to landward of the wharf; a warehouse was destroyed by oil bombs. One HE demolished the office and weigh-bridge at Newport coal sidings. Two HE fell in Calder's timber yard while one HE struck the LNER stockyard. One HE and 'over 100 IBs' fell in the Depot Road area; 'dozens of IBs landed on the Cargo Fleet graving dock, where they were promptly dealt with.' The North Tees power station suffered superficial blast damage when three HE exploded in the river, between the Synthetic wharf and the power house, and the Acklam Ironworks experienced splinter damage from one HE. During the course of the attack, storage tanks at ICI Billingham were set on fire, perhaps by incendiaries for a number of IB containers were subsequently found on the Britannia Works' site, just across the river from the chemical works. Whether there were casualties in addition to those already mentioned is not known.

**What is striking in this particular summary is the absence of any reported *civilian* damage in the vicinity of the Ironmasters' district, where the raid was concentrated. Down river, a number of IBs fell on the Surrey Street/North Street area of South Bank but their effects are not known.

25/26 July, 1942**
0047-0156hrs. Middlesbrough's most destructive air raid began at 0112hrs with the dropping of IBs in the area around the Scala cinema. Relays of aircraft dropped HE, oil-bombs, and hundreds of IBs, seemingly with the intention of setting the town ablaze. The Fire Brigade was soon heavily committed. This was the night that the Co-op Victoria Hall, at the junction of Clifton Street/Linthorpe Road was destroyed by fire and the Leeds Hotel, at the junction of Zetland Road/Linthorpe Road was demolished by a direct hit. When it was over, sixteen people had been killed and fifty injured; sixty-eight houses and seventy-six business premises had been destroyed, and minor damage had been inflicted upon c.1000 houses and 220 business premises. Notifiable industrial damage was officially described as 'negligible'.

28/29 July, 1942
2244-0020hrs. There was slight air activity over the Redcar/Eston area, during which one HE fell in Redcar and a number of IBs were scattered over the area. Two UXBs were subsequently found close to Coatham railway bridge, where they had caused some damage to the railway track. A number of HEs also fell on Eston Moor. It is believed that no casualties or significant damage resulted from the bombing.

3 August, 1942**

1250-1346hrs. At 1308hrs a low-flying Dornier 217 bomber, of II/KG40 launched four HE (each 500kg) at Middlesbrough railway station. Two HE scored direct hits on the station platform and track; one HE struck Kirkup's warehouse, Station Street, demolishing it and adjacent properties; one HE destroyed properties in Crown Street. Eight persons were killed and fifty-eight injured in the station, twenty-one of the injured requiring hospitalization.

6 September, 1942**

1138-1230hrs. At c.1145hrs two Me.210 fighter-bombers of 16/KG6 were intercepted off the Tees by two Typhoons of No.1 Squadron, Acklington. The raiders jettisoned four HE over Lackenby: two HE fell to the west of North Lackenby (one man was injured by a shrapnel splinter) and two HE dropped on Lackenby slag tip but failed to explode. No damage was caused. Both German aircraft were shot down: one at New Marske, the other at Robin Hood's Bay.

6/7 September, 1942

2325-0044hrs. Flares appeared over Middlesbrough at sporadic intervals from 2356hrs. Bombs fell at 0008hrs on 7 September: one HE on the LNER Goods' Yard; one HE on the Linthorpe Works; five HE and a number of explosive IBs which dropped on the Gresham Road/Vine Street area resulted in four dead (at 23 Gresham Road) and nineteen injured, including seven hospitalized cases. Fifty houses were seriously damaged and 180 people were rendered homeless. In other areas, twenty-eight explosive IBs were scattered across East Cleveland from Redcar to New Marske, while two HE fell on Grewgrass Farm, New Marske, and four HE dropped in the sea off Redcar beach. Sunderland was the designated target.

16 October, 1942

c.2140hrs. Flares were dropped over East Cleveland at 2131hrs and the first bombs followed nine minutes later. c.100 IBs dropped in the Borough Road/Redcar Lane district of Redcar and caused fire damage to two garages, two store sheds and four house roofs; one HE dropped at Black Bridge, Redcar Lane, and two HE at Ryehill Farm. Three HE caused blast damage to housing at Lackenby. At New Marske, four HE dropped south-west of Grewgrass Farm; one HE north-east of Pontac Farm and IBs were scattered from the farm entrance, along Longbeck Road to Horseclose Farm and the reservoir. Explosive IBs landed in the fields behind Marske High Street and HE dropped along the Saltburn Road nr Tofts Cottages. There was some blast damage to housing and farm buildings in the Marske/New Marske area but the only casualties were three cows injured!

12 December, 1942

0450-0552hrs. One UXB (believed to be 1,000kg) fell at Barnes Farm, Skelton and IBs dropped at Upleatham. No damage was recorded.

14 December, 1942

2010-2109hrs. There was 'slight coastal activity' over the Tees/Skelton district. Three HE were dropped on Cleveland Ironworks, Grangetown, and caused a temporary stoppage of the coke oven plant. Explosive IBs dropped in the Skelton area and HE fell on Warrenby Works. Total casualties numbered five killed and thirteen injured. It is believed that the dead included Samuel Brockley, Frank Hill, Thomas Hoskins and William Thompson – employees of Cleveland Ironworks.

17 December, 1942

2155-2250hrs. Explosive IBs were dropped in the region of RAF Upleatham, a *Starfish* decoy site to the south of Sandy Lane (which connects Dunsdale and New Marske). There was no damage or casualties. It was on this night that a returning Lancaster bomber was caught up in the raid and was shot down in error by Bofors' gunners at Warrenby. The entire crew of seven were killed when the plane crashed near Middle Farm, Dormanstown.

20 December, 1942

1920-2020hrs. There was slight enemy activity when one HE and one UXB fell in Wilton Avenue, Dormanstown, causing neither damage nor casualties.

1943

22 January, 1943

Time unknown. One HE exploded in a field between the river and the railway at Yarm (map ref. 898328), making a crater 20ft deep and 35ft across. There were no casualties.

3 February, 1943

c.2030hrs. IBs were dropped near Loftus and two HE near Scaling garage, the latter demolishing the living quarters of the garage and slightly damaging farm outbuildings. Two HE fell in fields at Tidkin Howe Farm, Skelton. Two HE and eight UXB were dropped on Lazenby allotments. Two HE fell between Low Farm and Wheatlands Farm, Redcar and one UXB was found along the Marske-Redcar road. A number of the UXBs appear to have been delayed-action bombs: they exploded the following day, including a 500kg bomb at Lazenby.

11/12 March, 1943**

2142-0014hrs. At c.2330hrs, after the dropping of flares over the Tees area (especially over Newport Bridge) for the preceding 15 minutes, three HE fell at South Bank. These landed near the police station, near the fire station and in Skippers Lane respectively. Two persons were killed and thirty-one injured (including eighteen hospitalized) at South Bank; ten houses and shop property were seriously damaged and 140 properties rendered uninhabitable and the Middlesbrough-South Bank road was blocked for two days. Two parachute mines dropped at Thornaby at 2333hrs. One landed near Five-lamps corner and one at the junction of Clare Street/Thornaby Road. There was extensive damage to property (including the demolition of the Britannia Hotel) in the latter area. A direct hit on an electricity sub-station also cut off power to a number of local industrial plants. Three persons were killed and seventy-five injured (including four hospitalized). One HE also fell at the junction of Lawrence Street and Yarm Lane, killing one man. Two HE dropped near Wreford's Farm, Newham Grange, but their effects are unknown. No bombs fell on Middlesbrough but three fire-watchers were seriously wounded (two fatally) in Westbourne Road, Linthorpe, when an anti-aircraft shell landed close by.

22 March, 1943
2235-2349hrs. IBs fell in the Grinkle Park/Scaling/Easington area and six UXB dropped into fields at Lane End Farm, Dissington. Eight HE, including three UXB, were dropped at Tockett's Farm, Guisborough. At Upleatham, two HE landed at Crow Well Farm and another (believed to be 1,000kg) fell at Holme Farm, seemingly without significant effect. IBs, including the explosive variety, were dropped over Upleatham, Wilton Lane and Barnaby Side Farm. In the Redcar area, three houses in Zetland Road were badly damaged by IBs; a large number of IBs fell on the beach at Warrenby Marsh; and four HE dropped into the sea just south of the South Gare. On the opposite side of the Tees estuary a number of IBs were dropped between the North Gare and the zinc works.